APPRENTICESHIP

Peter Gill

APPRENTICESHIP

OBERON BOOKS

LONDON

First published as hardback in 2008 by Oberon Books Ltd
First published as paperback in 2018 by Oberon Books Ltd
521 Caledonian Road, London N7 9RH
Tel: 020 7607 3637 / Fax: 020 7607 3629
e-mail: info@oberonbooks.com
www.oberonbooks.com

A catalogue record for this book is available from the British Library.

ISBN: 978-1-78682-406-6

To those who went before

To those who went before

Part One

WHEN I was moving house recently, I found a New & Lingwood shirt box containing a diary I had kept when I was a young actor with the Royal Shakespeare Company, during its first season at the Aldwych Theatre in 1962. I had joined the company to play Silvius in a transfer of Michael Elliott's celebrated production of *As You Like It*, with Vanessa Redgrave as Rosalind, from Stratford-upon-Avon to London, and to be in a new production – the first professional one in England – of *The Caucasian Chalk Circle* by Bertolt Brecht, directed by William Gaskill.

Brecht's impact, through the Berliner Ensemble, on the development of the European theatre after the Second World War, is almost forgotten now. The British theatre was a latecomer to this influence, not least for financial reasons. We didn't have the subsidies for the kind of theatre afforded in the rest of Europe where, in Italy and France, and particularly in Germany East and West, the effect of the Berliner Ensemble was as great on them as had been that of Ibsen and Wagner in the nineteenth century, because there were funds available there to finance it. We were also late to this table, in part out of native scepticism and wariness as well as from insularity and lack of cash.

The Berliner Ensemble's marked political and visual aesthetic, its company of accomplished and committed actors, the theory of staging and presentation it promoted and its attractive *mises-en-scènes*, stood for something that seemed very important to the British theatre at a time when it looked once again to be serious. The Ensemble's season at the Palace Theatre in 1956, which presented productions of Brecht's *Mother Courage* and *The Caucasian Chalk Circle* as well as an adaptation of Farquhar's *The Recruiting Officer* called *Trumpets and Drums*, had an immeasurably powerful impact here. It had a great effect on the way that the theatre looked at itself and it was an example of how theatres might be run on ensemble lines. It seemed to provide an ideal of theatre in a civilised world and one that could not be obtained on commercial terms.

The company epitomised too an aesthetic freedom, not only from boulevard values, but from the conservatism associated, on the one hand with the orthodoxies of socialist realism, and on the other hand from the conservatism of an art theatre that seemed out of date. This fitted well with the feeling of post-war British theatre which wanted to pack in its native philistinism while wanting to maintain its native empiricism and which felt robust enough to achieve this. The new sort of poetic realism that the Berliner Ensemble espoused chimed with the native temperament here.

Brecht was aware of the reservations and isolation of the British theatre, whose traditions he so much admired. In the last note he ever wrote to his company, he said *à propos* of the season:

For our London season we need to bear two things in mind. First: we shall be offering most of the audience a pure pantomime, a kind of silent film on the stage for they know no German. (In Paris we had a festival audience, an international audience – and we ran for a few days only.) Second: there is in England a longstanding fear that German art (literature, painting, music) must be terribly heavy, slow, laborious and pedestrian. So our playing needs to be quick, light, strong. This is not a question of hurry, but of speed, not simply of quick playing, but of quick thinking. We must keep the tempo of a run-through and infect it with quiet strength, with our own fun. In the dialogue the exchanges must not be offered reluctantly, as when offering somebody one's last pair of boots, but must be tossed like so many balls. The audience has to see that here are a number of artists working together as a collective (ensemble) in order to convey stories, ideas, virtuoso feats to the spectator by a common effort.

At the time of my diary, very few professional productions of Brecht had been mounted in Britain. The early plays and the poetry of Brecht were largely disregarded and undervalued everywhere, which ignoring led to an incomplete understanding of the later work which was then the most performed. There had been a successful commercial production of the Marc Blitzstein *The Threepenny Opera*, at the Royal Court Theatre in pre-Devine days, produced by Sam Wanamaker. Oscar Lewenstein had produced Joan Littlewood in a Theatre Workshop production of *Mother Courage* at a festival in Devon, and the Royal Court had produced *The Good Woman of Setzuan*. The RSC staging of *The Chalk Circle* was the first production of that play in Britain by professional actors.

I could account for the diary, but not immediately for the New & Lingwood box in which I found it, until I remembered Michael Fish, the Michael Fish who later opened a shop called Mr Fish, a chic, quintessentially Sixties establishment, where exquisite shirts in voile and crêpe de chine, together with kipper ties in silk and satin, were to be had as accessories to the wardrobes of the trendy young; that Michael was, at the time with which we are concerned, serving as a counter-assistant in Jermyn Street, first at New & Lingwood and then at Turnbull & Asser, two of the most conservative establishments imaginable, where he learned his trade and where, too, he occasionally landed his friends shirts and sweaters at cost price. In my case it was a grey cashmere sweater, which was expensive even at cost.

The combined images of the box and the diary made for a potent recollection of that time, a year before Philip Larkin's *Annus Mirabilis*, when the Fifties finally segued into the Sixties. A time when the world of Lita Rosa and Dickie Valentine and Alma Cogan and *The Billy Cotton Band Show* and the Royal Ballet and Bertorelli's and Chez Solange and Speakers' Corner and Ban the Bomb became one of the Beatles and the Rolling Stones and the King's

Road and Merce Cunningham and Rudolph Nureyev and *That Was The Week That Was* and colour supplements and Granny Takes a Trip and Lord Kitchener's Valet. There was an unreconstructed Tory party in government and a Clause 4 Labour party in opposition. The trades union movement was flourishing, the hereditary principle was safe in the House of Lords, convicted murderers were hanged, homosexuals lived outside the law, divorce was obtained principally by the well-heeled, racial equality was a leftist dream, the theatre was censored, contraception was primitive, and everything was on the cusp. Recreational drugs came then on prescription, with uppers and downers like Mandrax and Dexedrine as the favourites and with minor tranquillisers like Librium just making their way onto the scene. Reliance on dope and the use of LSD were yet to come. It was still a beer-and-cigarettes, a whisky-and-gin time.

It was a pre-time too for me, when my interest in directing and writing began finally to supersede my interest in acting, and the experience of being in Gaskill's production was very important to me, baffling and exhilarating and sometimes frankly awful, as the diary shows it to have been. I must have known that it would be significant for me, or willed it to be significant, to have kept a diary, who had virtually no aptitude for tasks of that kind. So that no matter how inarticulate and immature it, for the most part, is, the diary creates something of the frustration of a young actor trying to understand what the theatre is and in the process of understanding, moving towards becoming a director. Writing for me then was secret and automatic. The discomfort of reading the diary, and a certain satisfaction in having kept it, bring back some of the feeling of what it was like to be in those rehearsals at that time.

· · · · · ·

The Royal Shakespeare Company was then in its infancy. Peter Hall had taken over the direction of the company from Glen Byam Shaw in 1959, when it was still called The Shakespeare Memorial Theatre. It was renamed by Hall, in part as a tribute to Jean Villar's company, the Théâtre National Populaire – the TNP, the great French company, itself greatly influenced by the Berliner Ensemble – as well as being part of a modernising, rebranding exercise. It was during the run of *The Chalk Circle* at the Aldwych, in 1962, that permission was given to use the Royal title and the name of the company was changed, which seemed to some an odd thing to do for a company basing itself on socialist models.

But Hall was ever the pragmatist, and he would find himself well suited to Wilson's Britain that was to come. His political skills and drive were equal to his entrepreneurial ones. He turned a small, if successful and famous, festival theatre into an international one and he persuaded his chairman, Fordham Flower, to sell much of the property that the Flower family had secured for the company, and Lord Goodman's Arts Council to part with hitherto unheard of sums of money, all for this now royal and national company. The new name had, to more sophisti-cated minds than mine then was, the feel of a compromise worth making, a compromise which was, however, indica-tive of future policy at the RSC.

This was a period of trial and error for Hall, too. He was still experimenting with ideas of programming and with which actors, directors and designers suited his purpose for the company, until at last he settled on the collabora-tors who would help mount the cycle of history plays, *The Wars of the Roses*, which in 1964 really set the seal on the company. The nucleus of that acting company was already in place in 1962 and included actors like Roy Dotrice and Ian Holm and, most significantly, Peggy Ashcroft from the Byam Shaw Company, and would take into its number actors whom Gaskill had recruited for *The Chalk Circle*, as well as others still to come. But Hall's collaboration with Joan Littlewood's designer John Bury had not begun, although John Barton his Cambridge friend and close colleague had been on board from the beginning.

This production of *The Chalk Circle* was itself an indica-tion that Hall was also at pains to show how the company was set to play its part in a project that was underway else-where and which was presently engaging the progressive English theatre in a notable way, pushing it forward to reconnect with the ideas of Harley Granville Barker and William Poel from the past as well as with more contem-porary European ones. This project had been set in motion some years earlier by Joan Littlewood at Stratford East and by George Devine at the Royal Court.

This movement of regeneration was a reaction to the commercial theatre of the time which, even at its best, was still a hangover from the days of the bright young things, when the smart diction of writers like Somerset Maugham and Noël Coward had set the tone and a notion of aristocratic charm had been decked out by the considerable talents of Cecil Beaton, Oliver Messel or Rex Whistler. Straight plays then echoed the themes of Ibsen and Chekhov, recycled into airless statements of genteel distress. Even writers like Terence Rattigan could often do no more than write in code, and any transgression was a drawing-room rebellion. So that an insistence on notions of good taste ensured a numbing respectability. Even the grace of the work of Frederick Ashton, the pre-eminent choreographer of the time, sometimes became whimsical, and productions of Shakespeare at The Old Vic seemed part of this mood too, one which on stage seemed coloured by elegant futility and offstage had an air of an acceptable Bohemia, where Bloomsbury met Mayfair, the men spoke like Mountbatten, and familiarity with the Queen Mother seemed part of the chic.

There was a strong anti-queer element in the reaction to the theatre of the day, supported in some cases by a Marxist analysis of homosexuality as a bourgeois diversion, a capitalist infection (this was before the Frankfurt school of philosophers), as well as by ordinary British prejudice, with disdain for what it saw as outmoded bum-boy good taste. You had to be a very good gay actor to get work at Stratford East or the RSC or at the Court Theatre at that time, where some of the directors expressed the confusion of their sexuality in a confusion about what made something camp or frivolous. There is always something brutal in generational change, no matter how necessary. The flair of the men, mostly men, that I have just mentioned (Coward and Messel, etc) was not appreciated at this time and they were most of them in decline now from their own standards. If you haven't been in a weekly rep production of *Nude with Violin* or been to see *Variation on a Theme* at the then Globe Theatre, you won't really sympathise with how bad things had become, and however seemingly elegant the West End was, it was also dull, dull, dull.

There had been an attempt at West End seriousness of course, a worthy seriousness, coming out of Arnold Bennett and the Manchester school epitomised by JB Priestley, whose *An Inspector Calls* is a perfect example of the reality of the London theatre of the time, even in a serious play. *An Inspector Calls* was first performed in Russia in 1945. Its first London production was at the New Theatre, then the Albery, now the Coward, in 1946, and its effectiveness made it suit two very different orthodoxies. The tragedy of *An Inspector Calls* is one of a girl who has been forced into suicide by a middle class-family through the heartlessness of its individual members. Priestley dramatises this by leaving the girl out of the play altogether. She doesn't have any actual corporeal theatrical life at all and the tragedy dramatised becomes not hers, but the tragedy of the family which has destroyed her. The inclusion of the spectral Inspector makes it something of a cautionary tale, and its historical setting protects a bourgeois audience from anything but a worrying surmise. In Russia at this time its interpretation would have been conservatism of a different kind.

In the British theatre it seemed as if, between 1918 and 1945, nothing but the fears and miseries of the middle class had been dramatised, as if nothing of significance had happened to anyone who wasn't well-heeled. T S Eliot, whose early poetry had shown a natural feeling for what were often theatrical ideas, was reduced to writing West End trivia in a revival of poetical drama dominated by him and Christopher Fry. I was once in a revival of one of these verse plays called *This Way to the Tomb* by Ronald Duncan at, needless to say, the Arts Theatre. It had incidental music by Benjamin Britten and was unutterable tosh of a kind which abounded then, in an attempt to improve the tone of the more commercial theatre.

There were occasional productions of American plays and regular ones of whimsical French plays, for an audience still in awe of French culture. No one seemed to want to dirty his hands, certainly not on stage. There emerged too a brutal indifference to some of the excellences of what had gone before. Rodney Ackland, who had been so championed by Frith Banbury, was living in a West London Council flat. His play, *The Pink Room*, was so badly mauled by Harold Hobson in the *Sunday Times* that afterwards he wrote only adaptations, until he stopped writing altogether. He was disregarded by my generation or, when he came to mind, was presumed to be dead until the play was revived at the Orange Tree in Richmond in 1988, free of the shackles of critical disdain and of censorship, and renamed *Absolute Hell*. It proved to be as good a play as one written by Ödön von Horváth, a writer who incidentally had had no impact here at all at that time.

Great working designers like Leslie Hurry also found no place in the new theatrical world. Of course, the people who were seeking to change things hadn't been produced in a vacuum. They owed much of what they knew to those who had gone before, in particular to all the people working in a very strapped alternative theatre, which had struggled, since the days of William Poel and H T Grein, to say something about the contemporary world in the theatrical form. The perception, however, was still of a theatre that needed reform, and access to public money, no matter how small the amount compared to that available in Europe, made this possible.

There had been a perceptible shift in the class base in the theatre after the war so that the make-up of people engaged in this new enterprise was heterogeneous. In the new disposition, the actors trained in drama schools or in the repertory theatres, the designers were from art school, the technicians trained on the job and the writers came from everywhere. Necessary spin was provided by the directors, who were educated in the older universities. At the Court they were all from Oxford; at the RSC from Cambridge. Joan Littlewood was the single director at Theatre Workshop and she trained at RADA. Hall and Devine both took university backgrounds to be axiomatic for directors. John Dexter was the exception to the rule at the Court and Clifford Williams at the RSC, where he was an assistant.

One of Hall's aims was reclamation. Shakespeare was seen then partly as a festival playwright, not often performed outside the Old Vic or Stratford-upon-Avon. There were sometimes outstanding performances of the plays, but there was an air of gentility shrouding them too, something respectable. Performances of many of Shakespeare's plays were still a rarity, the three parts of *Henry VI* had only been seen in recent years once, at Birmingham Rep, in 1953. The modern-dress initiative had mutated, under the influence of the first great university director, Tyrone Guthrie, into something more eclectic, where the plays were often set in periods different to the one intended, in order to illuminate their intention and to make them more relevant and accessible. But in many productions this had descended into cliché and archness, where Nerissa played the virginals and Portia played with a bird in a cage and the girls in *Much Ado About Nothing* had shrimping nets or fishing rods or butterfly nets. There seemed to be either frivolous productions or worthy ones. The notional aim of the new RSC was to challenge the idea that Shakespeare was serious only in the study and to rescue him for the aims already in place in classical productions at the Court and particularly at Stratford East, these following on in spirit from Barker's famous productions at the Savoy Theatre.

I didn't enjoy my time at the RSC and couldn't identify with the work outside the two productions I was in. I think this was largely temperamental. It seemed to me to be too heavy and too pious and too worldly. Peter Hall and John Barton had a profound understanding and enthusiasm for Shakespeare but their theory of speaking seemed corseted by an addiction to formal emphasis, to an over demonstration of the iambic line and an insistence on marking the end of it. This approach didn't accommodate the fleet plasticity of Shakespeare and his eventual development as a writer of almost free verse. When the interpretive baggage and the shouting were added, it became too heavy-going, too depressed, too masculine. They directed as if by reading and not by hearing, as though their heads were in the book rather than watching and listening to the actors.

There was something else that didn't suit me, and I think that this was temperamental too: a mixture of academic seriousness with something much more opportunistic. F R Leavis was an important part of the Cambridge of this time. His belief in the moral dimension of literature influenced those reading English there, and indeed everywhere English was studied, and whether taught by him or not. An institutional tendency towards a sanctimonious justification of any falling-off from the balance struck between Leavisite virtue and theatrical pragmatism marked the RSC, then and later on, and led to many apparent anomalies which were in fact extensions of policy from the beginning; like the production of *Les*

Miserables in 1985, resulting in the subsequent tenden-
tious reappraisal of the musical by Cambridge graduates,
as if the form needed to be made respectable by them and
that the musical was hitherto without a proper imprima-
tur, and that Porter and Coward and Jerome Kern and the
rest had been waiting for the patronage of the children of
Doctor Leavis before they could become acceptable. The
production *of Les Miserables* at the height of the Thatcher
revolution has had as profound an effect on the subsidised
British theatre as *Look Back In Anger* had in 1956, and the
resulting cash-based populism has been led principally by
directors, mostly of course from Cromwell's alma mater.

I didn't find myself at home in the RSC company which
I found part rancorous and part arse-licking, and I was too
young and too inexperienced to understand the difficulty
of recruiting and maintaining a committed ensemble and
contending with actors as untutored as me. My particular
friend in the company, apart from Susan Engel whom I
already knew, was Paul Bailey. Like me, he was in transi-
tion, making his way from actor to novelist.

Our journeys home after the show often lasted till early
morning when, after hanging about in Soho pubs and the
few gay clubs that there were, we would end up in Marble
Arch where some of the habitués of Speakers' Corner
still were, who Paul delighted in. And anon west, Paul
to Bayswater and me to Hammersmith. Bailey's mordant
South London observations, over his Guinness, captured
the desuetude of the time; observations of its curious
anomalies, of poverty and an unimpressed examination of

the goings-on of our contemporaries, filtered through a sentiment for the odd and mysterious. Sometimes when I got home the tide would be up on the river, full in the early morning light. We neither of us, I think – certainly I didn't – appreciate then the difficulty of recruitment and of keeping loyal a large ensemble committed to working for long periods of time. And some of us were too self-concerned to make committed members of such a big company.

Susan Engel I already knew, and we saw a lot of each other then. There was a time when we used to read the stories of Chekhov together, and I later adapted a story of his called *My Life* in which she played the part of a girl in love with the hero. She had worked at the Court with Anthony Page and Gaskill, and she had been one of the first students on the newly designed drama course at Bristol University where she had been in the first production of a play by Harold Pinter: *The Room*. Gaskill's production of *The Chalk Circle* marked her debut with the RSC where afterwards she became part of the ensemble.

Engel's parents had left Vienna just before the war taking their infant children with them. I sometimes went with her to visit them in Bournemouth where something of Vienna was still to be enjoyed, particularly in her mother's kitchen which was quite un-English, and her personality too was different, like a Hampshire Marschallin. Mr Engel kept a picture of the Burgtheater in the sitting room, near the concert piano, where he imagined Susie playing Iphigénie. It was there that I met Rudolph Schwarz, who was then the conductor of the Bournemouth Symphony Orchestra. At lunch one day, when his sleeve rode up, I saw the tattoo from the concentration camp on his arm and I remember the shocking ordinariness of it and the unlikely combination of images of Hitler's Germany and Bournemouth hospitality. And in retrospect, how much Europe did in fact penetrate then our apparently hermetic world.

Peter Hall's management of the RSC also sought to emulate the notable success which George Devine had made with new writing at the Court theatre, so that eventually the company played its part in the establishment of writing being at the centre of the new order. Hall landed Harold Pinter as house dramatist. (It is interesting that he chose to woo Pinter at this time rather than Beckett, whose *Waiting for Godot* he had directed at the Arts theatre in 1956.) *The Homecoming* remains for me the high-water mark of the RSC's work, the first act seeming to me as powerful an image of an aspect of working-class family life as I had ever seen. The monumentalism of that production suited well the temperaments of Hall and Bury and Pinter. I'm not sure it suited the temperament of Pinter's play. The RSC played host to Peter Daubeny's world theatre season too, giving the company an international dimension.

●　　●　　●　　●　　●　　●

What was it that made me keep a record of that production, who had no talent for keeping anything so routine, for homework of this kind? I knew William Gaskill from working at the Court theatre as a young and junior actor, and he was a frequent visitor at the house in Hammersmith belonging to Sophie Devine, where I lived. I was drawn to his intelligence and to our common and complete devotion then to a somewhat un-English idea of art and particularly to the art of the theatre. This had something of the unabashed and complete enthusiasm of a schoolboy friendship where, outside any difference, you cleave to someone who sees the world in large part as you do, and this seeing corresponds to something deep within you – a chance and fateful bind almost outside the personal. There is a need to go to where you might be understood on a matter of taste and interest which often separates people out.

Gaskill's considerable analytic skill and rebarbative personality, his enthusiasm, his strange combination of the sudden and the rational, his plain speaking (descending into Yorkshire cliché with scant respect for the other people's feelings), a fear of being foolish and a total inability, strange in a theatre director, of being able to conceal his frequent boredom, his apparent lack of much worldly ambition combined with an astonishing sense of his amour propre, his singular moral courage and his hunger to be awkward at all times, made for an interesting and rewarding if bumpy time. We had all kinds of congruent taste and nearly always agreed, or were glad to be persuaded of something valued by the other.

We were both fond of the ballet then, which in London at that time was developing dancers of my generation of unusual skill and grace, but we were frustrated by it, by an art that has of necessity to be perfect if it is to succeed. We were great leavers-before-the-end of everything that fell short in the theatre, particular of ballets involving lovesick clowns. We were amazed at Ashton's *Symphonic Variations*, in fact amazed by all that master's work. We sat in a half empty Sadler's Wells to watch Tudor's *Dark Elegies* danced by the Rambert company to the *Kindertotenlieder*, then, like much of Mahler, hardly heard elsewhere. And once at the Jeannetta Cochrane to see Tudor's little *Triumph of Venus* to Kurt Weill's music.

We depended on American seasons in London for modern dance, where sometimes we met Harold Lang, an actor and teacher whose enthusiasm for modern dance led to his introducing Yat Malmgren to Gaskill. Martha Graham was a passion of his and his amazing and funny excoriations of much of what was current, particularly Tony Richardson's productions, were legendary. It seems strange to have been interested in an art so reliant on perfection, when what we aspired to influence was a form as human and fallible as the serious theatre is.

Perhaps I kept a diary because the production promised to be of interest simply because of the resources it had. The long rehearsal period for example and the big company were still relatively new things to be allotted to a contemporary play and it promised to be of interest because of this. But I think I kept a diary because the production was being undertaken at the outset with seriousness and in a spirit of commitment and enquiry which, as a 22-year-old, was what I wanted to be part of. That, as we used to say, or rather people more hip than me used to say, was where I was at.

I had been fortunate in the directors I had worked with so far, and maybe it was that which quickened my interest in following them. My first job was on a one-night-stand tour of *Look Back In Anger* and *She Stoops to Conquer*, to theatre-less areas, mounted by the Arts Council. My friend Anthony Hopkins and I had just left college, I after only a year of being there and he after two, and we were taken on by Frank Dunlop, who was directing the plays, as Assistant Stage Managers. I was just turning eighteen and the hetero hell of the Osborne play, which I was prompting and knew almost by heart, was foreign to me. I was fascinated by the invective, which I found so personal that it seemed to be somehow directed at me, as I sat in the prompt corner, listening to its curious, reactionary anguish and violence. If I had known what reactionary meant I might have felt insulated.

I had loved reading Oliver Goldsmith's *The Vicar of Wakefield* when I was young and it was Dunlop's attitude to *She Stoops to Conquer* that impressed me: his wanting to protect it, to celebrate it, to banish from the production any interpretation of the chocolate box or Gainsborough Studios kind. The designs were by Riette Sturge Moore, the sets taken from Turner, and the clothes from Stubbs. Dunlop's attitude was a development of his training at the Old Vic School, where Sturge Moore had taught, and where every aspect of the process of making theatre was understood to be important as part of making a play come to life.

Sturge Moore was, I discovered, the daughter of Thomas Sturge Moore, a poet I had come across in a volume of poetry of the Georgian school. My eighteenth birthday was marked by my first dress rehearsal in the theatre, and took place at the Unity Theatre, an amateur and socialist theatre in Goldington Street, Mornington Crescent, which, more than anywhere I came across afterwards, was full of the legendary smell of size and greasepaint and the heavy scent of face powder. I had been staying with my friend Stephen McKenna's family in South Harrow during the rehearsal period, commuting every day to work. The dress rehearsal finished so late that I could not get back. Sturge Moore invited me to stay with her in the house in Well Walk in Hampstead which had once belonged to John Constable and where she had met Yeats and all her father's famous literary friends. She was tall, with a cloud of white hair and big teeth, and always a Woodbine in her mouth. She was kind and hospitable in a way that the aspiring young in the world of theatre had reason to be grateful for, and to many women like her. Her house was the first I entered of the London *haut bourgeois bohème*. I found out much later that her uncle was G E Moore who had so influenced the thinking of people like Bertrand Russell and E M Forster and that, in effect, my first working night in London was spent in Bloomsbury.

The serious London theatre of the time found comfort in houses like that, with atmospheres like that, and women like that too – kind and clever and talented and effortlessly hospitable – in houses all over London. Their owners had incomes which might be small but were often fixed; people whose taste, and confidence in their taste, led them to live in parts of London which many of their class found too unconventional. In Hammersmith, or Strand on the Green, or Canonbury, or south of the river, beyond the pale to Knightsbridge and Kensington then, in areas which were compromised by proximity to poverty. Houses with white rooms, furnished often from the Caledonian market, and filled with *objets trouvés* and their owners' confidence in their own taste. Cornwall and the Suffolk coast seemed to be where they holidayed and the chosen Mediterranean country was France. These were hospitable, comfortable people of the intellectual upper middle class, or from more conservative middle-class backgrounds in the Home Counties. They eschewed the West End, where taste was more conventional and where carpets were fitted, curtains draped and designed, unconfident flats and houses which were too expensive and too parvenu for them. Their taste had a tribal eclecticism touched by the modern and infused with something like *gemütlichkeit*.

Sophie Devine, in whose house in Hammersmith I was living at the time of the diary, and her sister Margaret Harris had, with their friend Elizabeth Montgomery, worked under the name of Motley and had been among the pre-eminent young designers of the Thirties. They were of a generation which hated St Pancras Station and admired Battersea Power Station, and part of a movement that was housed not only around Gordon Square. Bloomsbury was only a particular expression of something common to all classes in Britain, in reaction to the late Victorian world. Devine had run a smart dress shop designed by Marcel Breuer. Margaret Harris was a friend of Charles Eames and his chairs stood in her studio below an Italian Renaissance mirror and cabinets full of model sailing ships. This taste, which was an admixture of French post-Impressionism and an English nostalgia for things comfortable, had a considerable effect on the tone of the theatre with its rueful belief that ghastly good taste was better than ghastly bad taste. Joan Littlewood lived in Blackheath. Jocelyn Herbert was born and lived on Chiswick Mall.

I lived for a time in the house of another of these women, Francesca Wilson, who had been notably courageous in fighting the corner of refugees before and after the war. She lived in Primrose Hill and filled the top of the house with refugees, then mostly Hungarian, and the basement with artists. In the room next to me was a young aristocrat called Vanessa Stourton who was trying her hand at sculpture then. She resolutely defied her upbringing and had run away from her coming-out dance. Her almost pitch black room was filled with little white maquettes. In another room was an Israeli painter called Yosyl Bergner, who gave me an etching of Jerusalem before he left for home.

I went straight from that job, with Frank Dunlop directing *She Stoops to Conquer*, to the Nottingham Playhouse, then in a tiny converted cinema in Goldsmith Street. The director there was Val May who had, like Dunlop, trained at the Old Vic School and showed a similar seriousness. May was a remote figure never to be seen backstage except sometimes on a first night. I found there that, although being an ASM on a tour of one-night stands had been tough, it had nothing on being an ASM for a season at the Nottingham Playhouse. This was light years away from the thinking that brought about the European health and safety regulation and in the course of the season each of the male ASMs was hospitalised by reason of accident or exhaustion. May's production of *She Stoops to Conquer* didn't inspire me in its aspiration as Dunlop's had, but in many ways May's was better, certainly more efficient, and I understood then the difference between having a vision and realising it, of talking and doing, of pitching and worth.

I had seen Michael Elliott's celebrated production of *As You Like It* at Stratford and had enjoyed it because it treated the play as if it could be seen as companion to the greatest of Shakespeare's plays and not as a festival romp. But when I joined the company I found that there was something of *The Golden Bough* about the production too. I remember at the end, before Rosalind's entrance, those of us on stage after Touchstone's long speech about the degrees in lying, listening as if in a trance, to a mysterious sound, as if we were with Ratty and Mole in the episode called 'The Piper at the Gates of Dawn' in *The Wind in the Willows*. A high mindedness too, which I found had a sort of religiosity, a kind of conservatism which didn't suit me. It was dominated by an oak tree on a mound, bare in the first half and in the second dressed with Disney leaves for summer.

One of the delights for me of being in the production was waiting with Max Adrian, who played Jaques, for our entrances in Act Five each night we played *As You Like It*. We two were always down early. I remember Max standing in the dark, his big fur hat at an angle, his doublet worn like a car coat, and wearing the one pearl drop earring. I remember him telling me on such a night that Laurence Olivier had asked him to join the new National Theatre company, where there was to be a new spirit of egalitarianism, personified in the billing. Billing was still hierarchical then. At the RSC, it was set out in three tranches to indicate status, where I found myself between John Gielgud and Hugh Griffiths. Max was rather suspicious of the change in things proposed by Olivier. 'Larry says that we will all play small parts as well as big ones,' he told me. 'Larry will play a leading part one night and a footman on another night.' He clearly wasn't convinced that things would, in fact, be like this. 'The only time Larry will play a footman,' Max went on, 'is when he is carrying John the Baptist's head in on a charger.'

We all wore make-up then, very little in the case of the younger actors. Max wore it more generously applied, especially around the eyes, which were covered in green shadow. It was a mark of the time that, after he went south of the river to join Olivier's company, the make-up was reformed, the eyeshadow went, and the billing was alphabetical.

Central to Elliott's production was Vanessa Redgrave who, as Rosalind, gave an outstanding performance free from the eccentricity and narcissism that, for some, marked her later work. She wore her height like a trophy and, while not particularly witty as Edith Evans must have been and whose recording of the part, with her father, Michael Redgrave, as Orlando, she generously acknowledged as an influence, she nevertheless showed herself to be an actress of outstanding ability and command. Graceful and committed, she was uniquely central to the production, which was odd because she had not been the actress originally intended. Her looks and her personality evoked the golden world that Elliott found located in the play and which she uniquely embodied. It was a breakthrough generational performance.

Elliott's collaborator at the time was another director, Caspar Wrede, with whom he had produced some notable television. They had mounted a successful season of plays in 1959 at the old Lyric Hammersmith with a group of friends all, with the exception paradoxically of Elliott, students of the Old Vic School. This was the basis of what later would lead to the Royal Exchange Company in Manchester.

But it was at the Court theatre that I observed at first hand the work of three directors who I found most understood something I was groping for. There was something about the attitude at Devine's theatre that I admired too and this was its frank assumption that it was important – not an establishment theatre and not alternative theatre either – an attitude about itself which it shared with Theatre Workshop at Stratford East. And I liked the free spirit and contentiousness of the directors: Anderson, Dexter, Gaskill, Dunlop, May and Elliott had seemed to come with Arts Council approval; the directors at the Royal Court certainly did not.

※　　※　　※　　※　　※　　※

The Court theatre might easily have remained a literary theatre, even under George Devine's stewardship, and have been forced to close after its first season, or stumbled on in a compromised way for a while and then been put away as another failed attempt at rescuing the British theatre from its general crassness, if it had not been for Devine's patronage of Tony Richardson and, through him, of John Osborne. Osborne's plays, with their almost punk refusal to conform to anything but their author's narcissism, set the cat among the theatrical pigeons and his success helped to keep the Court afloat in its early years. Richardson was Devine's associate and he made an interesting counterpoint to Peter Hall. He shared Hall's drive and ambition but his was more daring and less establishment. His remarkable flair and quite astonishing appetite for success and for the good life marked him out. There was an American dimension to his ambitions too and, although he was always a tonic to a constipated situation, he had an almost wearisome, wayward, show-business conventionality, so that it was of no surprise that he eventually ended up in California as the paterfamilias of the English enclave there.

The first production I saw of Richardson's was at the New Theatre, Cardiff, on the first night of Barry Reckord's play *Flesh to a Tiger*, with a young jazz singer called Cleo Laine in the leading part. And the first production I saw at the Court was Richardson's production of *The Chairs* by Eugene Ionesco, in which Joan Plowright gave an amazing performance as the old lady. Jocelyn Herbert and David Walker designed a very beautiful and evocative Goya production of *The Changeling* for Richardson at the Court. And later at the Queen's Theatre, in a season mounted by the Court, there was an all-star production of *The Seagull* which I enjoyed principally because of a performance of Trigorin by Peter Finch. But, apart from these, I didn't enjoy or admire Richardson's productions, which were seldom more than demonstrations of an enthusiasm – unachieved, lame, university productions at variance, it seemed to me, with a new idea of directing that he helped to promote at the Court. It was the idea of things rather than their execution that seemed to take up his energy and his considerable entrepreneurial flair. Like Hall and Pinter and Osborne, Richardson's private style was unlike the bourgeois bohemianism I mentioned earlier. It was all more defiantly new and smart and concerned with demonstrating success.

Devine gave up his directorial ambitions and, to a certain extent, his ambitions as an actor in order to enable others to fulfil theirs and, by this, to realise a vision for the Court that was in some measure created by them and the writers. It was his skill as a facilitator and his gifts as a teacher that allowed so many different talents to emerge and it was his combination of vision, together with what seemed to some to be a pedestrian insistence on simple professional conduct, that helped to condition so many diverse and often fledgling talents. His considerable stage management and administrative skills too gave the Court a stability that was vital to enabling it to flourish. For many years I kept a returned memo, written on by George in blue Pentel, which said, 'PG, please sign your memos. It is bad admin not to. GD'. He kept a tiny notebook, again in his own hand, in which he put daily the details of the advance and the matured bookings as well of details of the previous night's takings. But he too was part of the Court theatre abrasiveness, the rasping edge to his voice often giving things a bracing and uncomfortable tone. But he was by nature a collegiate man; a kind, sensitive, uncomfortable man.

Apart from Gaskill, the two directors whose work at the Court impressed me most were quite different – almost polar opposites. Lindsay Anderson was a product of the upper middle class, public school and Oxford. John Dexter working-class, elementary-school and repertory. But the difference didn't stop there. Both had served in the army: Anderson of course as an officer, Dexter as an NCO. Gaskill and Anderson owed their places at the Court to Richardson, Dexter to Osborne with whom he had been in rep in Derby. Anderson and Gaskill came as fledgling directors, Dexter first through stage management. Together they all three made a great difference to the Court; it is they who shaped its identity, after its initial years, by reason of their strong personalities and views, and by who and what they championed. They were central to its continuing success and influence. And it was through them that Devine's belief in a collaborative theatre was most effectively realised – difficult as all three were and abrasive as these collaborations could be. Collaboration that was far from matey.

Jocelyn Herbert set the standard of design at the Court. Indeed, she and John Bury at Stratford East were central to the change that came about in the theatre at this time. Both were uniquely suited to the demands of the new order of things. Both invested design in the theatre with a new seriousness and elevated, particularly the design of new plays, to a level of understanding that was different to what had gone before, bringing an astounding aesthetic to an area that had hitherto been treated with very little visual understanding. Herbert was a guiding light to all three directors, as was the Court's first casting director,

Miriam Brickman. Brickman was devoted to the work and to the actors and, in turn, she produced devotion in others. It may be this shared moral aesthetic that made the productions of these opinionated and egotistical men so lacking in vanity and self-regard.

The Court was never a writer's theatre in the sense of the writer having any power or influence outside what they produced. The writers' power lay in their plays and these directors were able to subsume their own considerable creativity in the cause of the plays, without losing any sense of themselves. Their best productions, while having enormous personality, were a synthesis of talents, all informed by each one's temperament. Anderson, Dexter and Gaskill had, too, the guts to acknowledge that, creative as they were, however much they perhaps knew, it was the writers, no matter how limited they might be, who were saying things beyond directorial daydreaming. In the case of Dexter, his productions of five of Arnold Wesker's plays were simply outstanding, on a par with anything Brook or Littlewood or Guthrie ever achieved, completed within limited resources and like great pieces of expensive European *mise en scène*.

Anderson's most typical production was of David Storey's play *The Changing Room* which is set in a northern rugby league's changing room before, during and after a match. This was the most achieved and most expressive example of the collaboration between Anderson, Storey and Herbert, and it was cast to perfection by Anderson and Gillian Diamond. Without sacrificing any of the author's recollection of the reality of the afternoon, they created between them an almost metaphoric image that was a tribute to maleness and the male form, with male violence relegated to the pitch. Any accusation of it being a mere homophile tribute was kicked into touch by the scene in the dressing room, while the first half is being played outside, between the club chairman and the caretaker. These were played with exquisite judgment by Paul Dawkins and John Barrett, with a kind of a beauty at variance with the beauty of the players.

All three directors put the art of the actor high in their understanding of the theatre and central to any attempt to stage often fragile new plays that had no more to them than quality of tone or purpose. The discussion of acting, or rather of actors and their particular qualities, was part of the everyday talk at the Court, an almost ideological touchstone. The notion that any production calling itself serious could be obtained without a proper understanding of the importance of acting was thought risible. And what was understood, too, was the importance of the art of particular actors and not of some transferable system of acting. The art of actors raised to an almost philosophical idea. And it was under the combined enthusiasm of Devine, Richardson and these three, and later Anthony Page, plus a succession of gifted casting directors, that this particular attitude to acting and its relationship to directing was observed by a young actor working at the Court then.

Devine's dreams of a permanent company at the Court were soon dashed by financial constraints and, although there remained at the Court a belief in the efficacy of a Company, more *ad hoc* methods of casting became the order of the day, requiring a particular talent and a strict attitude to the marketplace if standards were to be maintained.

The ideal of a well-rehearsed company as the basis for a serious theatre was a common one then, a kind of tokenistic idea. In *I'll Go to Bed at Noon*, Stephen Haggard's book written for his sons before he went to the war – where he was mysteriously killed, found dead in a railway carriage in north Africa with no apparent explanation – there is expressed, the longing of his generation for a more committed theatre of this kind. Haggard was a successful and sensitive actor who had turned down a career in Hollywood. He corresponded with Barker and with Stanislavski, and was part of a group of young artists and friends, which included George Devine, who saw the ensemble as part of any new order.

There was too at the Court, and at the RSC and Stratford East, an impulse to dismantle the star system, but at the Court then there was no puritanical attitude to stars, only a disdain for poor acting and stars in the wrong parts. All three directors, Anderson, Dexter and Gaskill developed an affection for actors of varying types. Older established actors often found themselves revered at the Court in a way more tender than they found elsewhere. Quality was the watchword as far as actors were concerned and this was often very subjective. There was sometimes an almost over refined, hair-trigger approach to acting at the Court, in the search for quality, that marked it out.

Shop floor attitudes to actors differed between these three directors. Dexter sometimes descended to bullying and Gaskill could unnerve his actors with dis-incentive. Anderson never did this, and found directing actors of differing status easy, in spite of very particular enthusiasms. He didn't have a natural feel for producing performances of note from actresses, as Gaskill did. And Dexter did not have Anderson's refined and personal approach to actors, nor Gaskill's personal if eclectic and eccentric one. But all three were instrumental in the development of many young, often difficult actors, and in rescuing the reputations of many older ones.

•   •   •   •   •   •

The production of the Berliner Ensemble which particularly impressed the Court directors at this time was *Die Mutter*, Brecht's adaptation of Gorky's novel, which they went to see in Paris. This production seemed to crystallise for them certain things about the Berliner Ensemble that they understood in relation to the work they were undertaking at the Court. It may be something very English about it too: its elevation of the everyday into the poetic, its kindliness rather than its Bolshevism, and an imperative to take realism beyond demonstration and indication.

Dexter was the master of this. His having been in weekly rep for longer than anyone else at the Court seemed to have had two effects on him. He despised the glib external short cuts – the legendary directions to 'Cheat upstage, dear heart' or to 'Piss off downstage old boy' – but more than the others he retained a strong respect for some of the creative efficiencies of rep, particularly with managing time. And he was possessed of an immense passion, his coal-black eyes signalling obsession for particular people and for ways of doing things.

There was something in the English understanding of realism that helped to shift the Stanislavskian principle from the emotional life to the material idea. All three directors understood this, but it was Dexter who achieved most the necessity for a fulfilled material existence on stage. All of them understood the clarity of narrative and purpose that could come out of realised physical life, and something of the erotics too: a sensuality which would support plays that did not always fully achieve their aim, and invest them with a palpable sense of being.

While Devine's Court was inspirational for diversity, its chief and most original achievement had been prefigured by DH Lawrence before the First World War. Lawrence's plays have been appreciated after a fashion in England but in Europe hardly at all. There is a presumption that he was a mere realist, part of a Fabian project, an offshoot of the Manchester School, a liberal idealist, a by-product of the Antoine school of realism, somehow an addendum to Zola and Hauptmann.

True, Lawrence was perhaps influenced by the Irish theatre in his plays, but he was not interested in the overtly poetical, the versification of the Irish theatre and its satirical fun-poking. He projected the figures, particularly of the young working-class women he portrayed, as unequivocally themselves, as much the centres of their dramas as Hamlet is of his. He wrote outside the European idea of realism and outside the class base of Ibsen and Chekhov and the others. He was as much a revolutionary in attitude as that other playwright disregarded in his time, Georg Büchner, but perhaps less photogenic than he. The domestic canvas of Lawrence's three best plays leads to a misunderstanding of his achievement, and the lack of a proliferation of scenes, the absence of parasols and middle-class melancholy, make him inimical to many old European directorial vanities. There is something in the essentially English talents of a playwright like Lawrence, a poetic, almost palpable, recreation of being, that is at variance with the more abstract impulse of much of the modern European theatre. Certainly in the Expressionist movement, which appeared to be set in opposition to what a writer like Lawrence was trying to say to a theatre that would not listen. The Expressionists felt that they had something to record that was outside the scope of realism, something that Strindberg had been the first to address early in the 1890s, though no one called an Expressionist laid claim to the name.

But what is Expressionism? I am using the term generally, taking in a variety of manifestations of the modern period, and not in a textbook way. I mean a movement in art which is not only a reaction to the First World War but something arising at the end of the nineteenth century, a spirit that was intensified after the First World War. I mean Expressionism as part of Modernism but a particular tone of it, rising from the need to show the hidden in a more explanatory, more demonstrative, more overt way. A cruder way, if you like, than was obtained by the realistic school of the nineteenth century. A way that was most typified perhaps by the anti-realistic theatre of Meyerhold, who had been a pupil of Stanislavski, for whom he had created the part of Konstantin in Chekhov's *The Seagull.* This was a theatre which was emphatically and deliberately anti-illusionist. There is a portrait of Mayakovsky by Boris Grigoriev which captures something of the elegant grotesquery associated with him, portraying him double, both selves apparently dancing, one in bright oriental dress the other like a white gloved, top hatted master of ceremonies of the jazz age. Later, in Germany after 1918, Expressionism is typified in works like *Nosferatu* and *Metropolis* and in *The Cabinet of Doctor Caligari* – films much loved in art schools – and in the plays of Mayakovsky or Toller, where characters are abstractions rather than representations of recognisable people. If the music and painting of the time seem to have different resonances, it is perhaps because their nature is more formal and susceptible to the Expressionist idea. The dark, relentless expressiveness in, for example, Schoenberg's *Verklärte Nacht,* where an idea of feeling discovered in the opening bars of the slow movement of Beethoven's Ninth symphony seems to find an overwrought end. Later, the disturbed romanticism of Berg's operas is a thing of a different order. In painting, too, the exuberance seems more natural, even though the marvellous vitality of, for example, Kandinsky's paintings can seem just as potent in reproduction as in the gallery.

European Expressionism first of the 1890s and then, after the 1914-1918 war, did not take root here for reasons of resource and will, of national culture and censorship, as well as of timidity. The reformed form of it by the Berliner Ensemble struck a different chord here than in the rest of Europe. We have always had a longing for and a suspicion of something that seemed anyway unobtainable, and our tradition of expressing the hidden or implicit has been different, often within the anarchy of comedy – as in Lewis Carroll or Oscar Wilde – or in a taste for anthropomorphism.

In the 1920s, Terence Gray made a fist of Expressionism at the Cambridge Festival Theatre, and Peter Godfrey programmed many of the new European Expressionist plays at the Gate Theatre in Covent Garden. There was something of expressionism, too, at the Abbey Theatre, Dublin, and in the plays of the poets, particularly of Auden and Isherwood. But theatrical Expressionism is essentially a directorial tool and its attraction is aesthetic coherence of a different kind to that espoused by Barker, in his seasons at the Court theatre and the Savoy in the early years of the last century. Many of the stylistic devices which at first seemed exhilarating eventually became outmoded and were seen as simply rhetorical and exhausted. Joan Littlewood and Ewan MacColl were much influenced by the Expressionist movement in their early work together in Manchester, and something of it survived in the work of Theatre Workshop at Stratford East, where it was intertwined with ideas of popular theatre and with the ideas too of Stanislavski.

Expressionism in the Twenties, and particularly in the Thirties, was linked with the political concerns of the time, particularly with the anti-Fascist struggle in Europe, so that Auden and Isherwood, MacColl and Littlewood, and others on the left here – the majority of whom were working in mostly uncelebrated provincial or amateur and alternative theatres – were expressing fellowship with the anti-Fascist struggle in Europe. Although the communist party in England did not in fact approve of Littlewood and MacColl's approach to their work.

The Expressionist spirit in Germany and Russia is a much more complex phenomenon than is easily grasped. It not only characterised the work of some of those struggling against oppression, it also expressed the spirit of the oppressors, both in Russian and Germany, particularly the lurid, poster-like, unspecific element of Expressionism which suited both the Nazi and the Soviet view of things. There is something of nationalist Expressionism in Nazi propaganda in, for example, Leni Riefenstahl's film *The Triumph of the Will*. In Germany and the Soviet Union, the ruling elite's hatred was for Modernism in general perhaps, more than Expressonism, seeing in the former a bourgeois individualism that they thought was a diversion from the task in hand. Aspects of Expressionism seemed to have come naturally to Nazism more than the purer aestheticism of Modernism.

In the whole modern movement the difference between fancy and imagination, between something that has an authentic imaginative bite and something that is merely contrived, is difficult to judge and continues to be so even now in post-modern times. After Picasso's *Les Demoiselles d'Avignon*, in which he sought to forge something new out of where he felt Matisse had been leading, and in the movement following the Dadaists, it is difficult for anyone but members of an increasingly powerful elite to easily evaluate art outside museum aesthetics and financial gain. Fine art is in the hands of punditry that is more powerful and plausible and intellectually kitted out than obtains in the serious theatre, where profits are not so substantial and comment is more asinine. It may be that its relative lack of celebrity may make the theatre more fit for change.

In the contemporary theatre, much of the debate has been around concepts of what realism is and what it stands for. Is what is meant by realism a lazy, dull approximation of the surface of things, an unexplored, undigested compromise that is concerned with the eccentricities of the individual? Recordings, as it were, of things overheard on the bus, sensational stories of the lower orders, middle-class observations of the proletarian zoo. Or is realism an analysis of life, dramatised according to a socialist dialectic by means of selecting characters that are at once believable

and yet typical, credible but secondary to the purpose –
characters that are to an extent types, like those of the
Commedia, of Jacobean comedy, or in the French comedy,
a realism put to the purpose of demonstrating proposals
for change on political lines? Or is there something else to
realism, which is maybe more difficult to pin down, the
realism found in what the American writers like O'Neill,
Miller and Williams or Beckett, Brecht and Horváth have,
in their different ways, been attempting?

There is a class element in the continued attack on
realism in the theatre and this has something to do with
a new embarrassment, with the seeming uncoolness of
privilege when set against the implications of what realism
embodies.

The historic imperative of art to be concerned with
both truth and beauty, as an offering to the gods of the
best, always involved a tendency to separate out the refined
and the unrefined. Scatology in the Greek plays is pretty
well specific to the Satyr plays. Later, in the medieval
period and then in the Renaissance it is consigned to the
lower orders, which eventually influences notions of what
refinement is perceived to be and where it is located in
the modern world. And with this comes an idea of seem-
liness coming out of the Enlightenment, combined with
notions of eighteenth-century French taste and with sensibility confused with manners. This means that refinement
becomes a question of class – particularly with a notion of
aristocracy – projected by mostly bourgeois artists, and of
feelings that are rarely associated with the poor, except in

a pastoral sense. So realism eventually becomes associated with the sociology of class and invites the audience to take part in Orwellian distress, a sort of girls' boarding-school evaluation by smell, as if realism would inevitably imply a description of sanitary conditions, particularly of women, with realism itself becoming unseemly.

There is a difference between northern and southern Europe here. The northern Reformation leads to an attachment to godliness, involving cleanliness without the more Italian sensuality and corporeality. A puritanical realism on the one hand and a yet a fear of its implications on the other. The baser element of life noticed by an absence of reference to it.

This absence eventually leads to a belief that sensibility cannot co-exist with poverty. However, complicity with French taste of the *ancien regime* is not felt to be a cool reaction to the realistic idea, so more elaborate means of subterfuge are required, which is where a resort mythology can still come in handy. As if in counterpoint, there are some *soi disant* realists colluding in all this, supposing that lack of refinement is the *sine qua non* of truth, leading to programmatically soulless observations of a documentary world.

Realism suggests that while fine art, and particularly music, are able to ascend into a purely aesthetic world, and that while the theatre can aspire to states of music it is most certainly not music. Modernist abstraction is closed to literature, and particularly to the theatre, by reasons of their natures and destiny.

All debate in the modern theatre resolves itself around the figure of the actor. Any desire to replace him by more comprehensive means, by anything more than directorial authority, have proved interesting but so far barren, except in some vivid cases by means of puppets and the figure of the author himself taking part. Post-Isadora Duncan there has been a search for abstraction based on the human figure in dance, but even then it is sometimes difficult not to make human stories out of human figures, inspiring though the attempts have been.

And it is around this resolutely human form that there have been conducted some interesting experiments in the post-modern fine art world, where the artist has ventured in to what is in fact dramatic territory, seeing himself as performer or subject, to indicate directions that drama can take. Many of the more sculptural ideas and installations speak of human absences and there has been an interesting replacement of the human with the animal, or with the author's body, a corporeal concern with incident and with process through time that is intrinsically dramatic. Even abstraction at its most potent, in its realisation by the great Abstract Expressionists, was always going to be reminded of an observable reality and the existence of Campbell's soup cans.

Promiscuous Expressionism in the theatre, no matter how attractive, seems now to be an exhausted idea and not able to address the things it was perhaps designed to express, important things. To those who witnessed its transferral to Hollywood films and to Cyd Charisse caught in a wind-tunnel, there is something inescapably kitsch about it. It becomes everything it sought not to be and resembles the vacuous beauty of Powell and Pressburger films and interpretations of cinema as a branch of pop art rather than as narrative or drama or concerned with ideas – ideas beyond journalism. And the American musical has fed off the tropes of Expressionism so that the film and the musical theatre have homogenised these things. The classic Expressionist plays are simply not of the best, they are more concerned with what they are *not*, rather than what they are, with not being something, rather than achieving what they should be. They found little use for the art of the actor and seem empty to a theatre that needs more than stylistic devices.

There is still a nostalgia for a directorial theatre of a kind that was for a time challenged and set aside here, partly because of history but also because post-war ideas had led to a more modern concept of directing plays. At the Court theatre, those ideas led to something different. I worked some time ago with a Czech-born actress, Hanna Pravda, and asked what her memory of acting in Prague as a very young woman was: 'We spent our time on raked stages, one foot up and one foot down, always at angle.' She imitated acting on a wonky rake. '*You* are getting it now,' she said, referring to some production in the Lyttelton theatre. She was talking about mere Expressionism, a limp copying of the German state theatre of the 1970s. And yet it remains an apparent need. It's a puzzle.

● ● ● ● ● ●

When D H Lawrence's plays were revived at the Court at the end of the Sixties, they seemed curiously part of the Devine project, as if they had been written for that theatre. Devine's Court projected the lives of ordinary people, in their tragic or comic situation as the case was, in high definition, and in *mise-en-scènes* that were sometimes almost contemplative and disquisitionary rather than didactic. These plays were quite unlike anything conjured up by mere realism, since they had a poetic un-fustian dimension. And they found the actors to play the characters depicted, actors previously consigned to supporting others, shouting 'Chocks away!' in execrable films telling us how resolutely their betters had won the war.

I think, too, that there was a sophisticated understanding at the Court of the fragile nature of some of the writing. Part of the art of the theatre is contained in the subject dramatised and the directing was geared to this and often misunderstood because of its resolute refusal to conceptualise itself. Opposite views could be held: one, that Thomas Hardy had done something remarkable in writing *Tess of the d'Urbervilles*, for example, and the other that Henry James' dismay at the standard of the writing was understandable, and that both ideas could be acknowledged.

The Court put the cause of the new play at the centre of the theatre where it has stayed for 50 years. It also collapsed the idea of both the conventional structures coming after

Ibsen and some car-crash alternative, obtaining something different and more original. It would have been logical, after the experiments of the 20th century, that the director as author would prevail, something coming out of performance art that was new. But that has hardly been the case. I think it is because of failure of nerve and a misunderstanding of destiny as opposed to opportunity. The result has been directorial cannibalism, with the writer implicated, finding romance in working as it were on the floor of the rehearsal room. The courage demanded by collaborative theatre is difficult to obtain and in England perhaps we have the European theatre we deserve rather than the one we wanted.

Devine's theatre understood the relation that directing should take to new writing. Initiatives towards new plays which are essentially directorial and dramaturgical, seeing the writer as an adjunct and putting them on a par with the writer in films, were not part of his project. The confusion with, or envy of, film is unproductive; film is a quite different medium. The theatre director does not have the same relation to his collaborators on the technical side as does the film director, he has none of the dependence that the film director has on his cameraman and his editor, which makes him more exposed and which may be why so many directors in film have come from the theatre and none the other way.

The practicalities are different, and the insistence on the sole authorship of a film being the director's is partly a fiction too. Film and television production, no matter how punditry would have it otherwise, are largely in the hands of accountants, which is such a hard fact to acknowledge that it is of course never the cause of comment. The undoubted importance and sometimes pre-eminence of the director, particularly in film and increasingly in the theatre, has given the untalented a bogus view of things. The dramaturgical theatre as it is practised today is really a re-stating of old values, often coming out of the commercial theatre. It has become a branch of a literary philosophy that makes the director an extension of the critic and, like the critics, almost becoming in effect a Stalinist arbiter of what things are or should be.

Wilson Barrett, the Victorian actor-manager interviewed for the *Daily News* in 1885, says that 'dramatic authors are mistaken in finishing off a play and expecting to direct its entire production themselves without reference to scenic effects and many other things which go to the success of a stage play together with a good plot, striking situations and telling dialogue. I wish to urge this with all modesty but I think that the people who do the work of production can often help the author very much after he has invented his motive or main spring.'

When the young Robert Morley wrote his first play, he sent it to Marie Tempest, the most famous actress of the day. The play concerned a failed actress past her first youth. Tempest said she would take the play and put it on provided the character she was considering was made successful, since she couldn't play a failed actress. Morley obliged and Tempest put it on. These are not random examples. Wilson Barrett was an actor-manager of the old kind, a contemporary of Irving's. His company was based at the Prince's Theatre where he was famous for playing in Henry Arthur Jones' melodramas and for mounting a spectacular production of *The Way of the Cross* stolen from the better-known *Quo Vadis*.

Marie Tempest was a famous musical comedy star when young and later became a supreme light comedienne, famous for her charm. She even had a door-hinge named after her. The Marie Tempest was much used, particularly in rep, and is a hinge which stops the opened door wherever the artist wants it to stop, without it banging back. This enabled Tempest to make her characteristic first entrance though a French window, carrying flowers, unencumbered by fear that the door would come back on her. By this means she was free to acknowledge her audience. She made an entrance like this in Noël Coward's *Hay Fever*.

These were successful talented artists and powerful ones too who knew everything about theatre but probably not much about life, as perhaps did the authors they were in fact censoring.

This is not to say that dramaturgical intervention, play doctoring, is never in order or useful or necessary: Oscar Wilde's four-act version of *The Importance of Being Earnest* was doctored by George Alexander. Alexander was the manager at the St James theatre where he put the play on, after the failure of Henry James' *Guy Domville*. He created the part of Jack Worthing too, and later spurned Wilde, after his imprisonment. In the matter of *The Importance* he persuaded Wilde, for example, to cut a scene in Act Two, when a solicitor came to take Algernon Moncrieff back to London to face his debtors. Alexander saw this as extraneous and too detailed an account of Algy's profligacy to suit the comedy. His suggestions benefited the play, which was a much more worked-on text than Wilde tried to pretend, as the typescript manuscript of the version, called 'Lady Lancing', reveals.

In another context, the revising and editing that Ezra Pound did on T S Eliot's *The Waste Land* is as masterly as it is sensitive. It seems to me to depend on whether editors and play doctors in the subsidised world are as skilful as Alexander or Pound, and not versions of Barrett and Tempest with a belief that interference is a *sine qua non*. But it seems that the idea of singularity on the one hand and collaboration on the other, which was the project certainly undertaken in the 20th century, has been abandoned in favour of producer and directorial imperatives.

The presumption that no one had fulfilled the role of the director before the end of the nineteenth century is a false one, but the emergence of the director as a separate phenomenon was new and inevitable and necessary for coherence, if for nothing else. A comparison with the conductor in classical music who had emerged some decades earlier is inevitable but the idea of the director as a potential author marks a difference between the two mediums. European classical music has had a quite different development to the theatre. Even the celebrity conduc-

tor doesn't make the claim to authorship that the theatre
director now does, as a matter of course.

The personality of the Court was peculiarly mobile, by
turns nurturing and abusive. It was encouraging and
supportive to a degree but full of English suspicion and a
scepticism that was no more than a cutting-down-to-size,
with a disdain of intellectual pretension that was often a
front for timidity and good taste, and a kind of schoolboy
embarrassment and sneering and envy that are signatures
of an Oxford and Cambridge education. Only Bill Gaskill
went on to run the Court, soon after he and Dexter had
helped Olivier get the National Theatre off the ground,
bringing with them some of the Court's practicality and
daring, which had made its opening seasons so good.

Lindsay Anderson had started as a critic, and part of
him remained one, sniping at everything from the circle of
wagons he drew around any production he did, often influ-
encing events for which he subsequently took no responsibility, and seeming not to want to get his hands dirty
by putting himself forward to run the Court, as certainly
anybody running a theatre must. He was a considerable self-publicist and this created an image of his work,
certainly in the theatre, that was greater than that which
he achieved. Paradoxically, this led to an underestimation
of how good his work could be, partly because he often
opted for whimsy as a way of dealing with the difficulty he
found in the world of particularly, film, where he wasn't
indulged as he was in the theatre. John Dexter was never

seen as a contender to run the Court. He was the only one I never heard speak disloyally of Devine. The eventual defeat of Devine's Court was in part due to Gaskill and Anderson's failure to make common cause and a result of their often thuggish behaviour towards each other and to other people, and so that fire was put out.

But through all this there was a purity of purpose at the Court, a puritan burn and an almost platonic idea of what the production of a play should be. Of all the theatres I have worked in, it remains for me the one where an idea of a serious theatre prevailed over individual ambition. There was also a sense of family at the Court and of loyalty to its members, particularly on the outside, and often a remarkable gentleness to a young director who never needed to feel that his actors would be undermined or fear of another director giving notes. I think perhaps it was in some ways a therapeutic community, able to hold in their anxiety some pretty rackety characters and offer them some stability, and perhaps it was as good a way as any of processing unhappiness. It was like a family that was at once morbidly dysfunctional and yet amazingly competent.

Deference played its part at the Court. Devine was Mister to most of the staff, but conversely deference to the older apparently humbler members of the staff was marked. Deference to, or rather respect for Miss Gelder, who managed the circle bar, to the usherettes in their black frocks and white aprons, who served tea and Dundee cake in the interval of matinees, to Stan at the stage door, who lived in one of the cottages behind the theatre owned by the Cadogan Estate, and particularly to Lena Cope and to Elsie Fowler, secretary and housekeeper respectively. Lindsay Anderson once complained loudly of the noise made by the cleaners in the auditorium during one of his rehearsals, to find himself reprimanded by Fowler on the grounds that she had to do her work as much as he had to do his, which resulted in an apology from Anderson of a kind never offered by him in any other circumstance or anywhere else. And lest this sound like a play of manners by well-tutored middle-class boys in some mode of flannelled reparation, I must emphasise that this was not so. There was genuine sweetness to this side of the Court theatre and there was fun too. The spirit of comedy always made its way through the interstices of strife, on and off stage, in Sloane Square then.

Part Two

I WONDER NOW how Anderson or Dexter would have managed a production of *The Caucasian Chalk Circle* for the RSC in 1962. Anderson would certainly have made a sensitive, well-rehearsed job of it, although its epic nature might have proved tough for him then. He hadn't done many productions, nor yet directed a feature film, and though he was confident, he didn't have the experience of the theatre that Gaskill and certainly Dexter had, even though he was older than they were. He had a typical disdain for the technical skill that a production of a play like *The Chalk Circle* required. He wasn't interested in the theatre in that way and when he stepped outside the bounds of the poetic realism that marked his best work, as he often wanted to, it didn't seem natural to him. Anderson would never have been able to tolerate working for the RSC. He wouldn't have been able to compromise in the casting or have been comfortable with how Hall saw things. He would never have been able to cut the necessary deal; just as he was later unable to cut the deals necessary for making films.

Dexter would certainly have made a fist of the play and any production by him would certainly have been exciting and would have avoided a subsequent tendency for directors to see Brecht as a proto Robert Bolt. He would not have engaged, as Gaskill did, in an attempt to find out what it actually was that Brecht was after, and his production might have been more like Shaw than Brecht. It was this investigation by Gaskill to find out that remains interesting to me.

There were two methods of work that Gaskill concentrated on at the outset of rehearsals of the *Chalk Circle* – one was concerned with masks and character, the other with an approach to acting that was sympathetic to Brecht's intentions and to his approach to the theatre.

The masks to be used in the production were comic or character masks derived from the commedia dell'arte and the French character comedy deriving from this. The technique for using them was one taught at the Court theatre by George Devine, who had learned it from Michel Saint-Denis, who had in turn learned it from his uncle, Jacques Copeau. Copeau was part of the anti-anti-realistic movement seeking to reconnect with what was perceived as the origins of theatre practice and which came about in Europe as a reaction to directors like Stanislavski and Antoine. Copeau had devised the technique at the Vieux-Colombier, the theatre which he founded as part of this movement. It was used in the training at the Old Vic School in London, where Devine had worked with Saint-Denis, and it was a branch of comedy which much interested him. Devine had demonstrated this way of working with masks to the Royal Court Writers Group, run by Gaskill and Keith Johnstone, which resulted in John Arden's play *The Happy Haven* which Gaskill had directed.

The play concerns the power struggles of the inmates of an old people's home and their reaction to the elixir of youth being developed by their doctor. It is a resolutely anti-realistic work, Jonsonian in style, in aspiration influenced by Brecht's *Lehrstück*. The writing is strangely literary while the masks, the songs, and the insistence on open staging seem fanciful and external, so that in spite, or possibly because, of its good intentions, and the real ale side of it, it is unfunny. But it is an example of one side of the Court theatre that was central to Devine's policy.

In the century-old revolt against Ibsen there has been a common desire in the theatre to find the new through an examination of the old, often in an extension of the pastorals found in the Latin poets and in the Renaissance and the Enlightenment. In a search for authenticity and metaphor, a kind of romance has been found in idealising the popular while ignoring the poor, by revisiting the modes and affectations of the past while ignoring how they came about. The French theatre has been ideally suited to this, since in part it grew out of the tradition of the old Italian comedy which came to France in the sixteenth century when the harlequin and the clown established themselves as useful figures in dramatising or masking what were often courtly or bourgeois values. An idealisation not only of the world of the commedia but also of the circus and the cabaret have figured in French painting since Watteau, particularly in Lautrec and Degas. In the French theatre this is present from Marivaux down to Beckett and Barrault, Marceau and Lecoq.

And not only in France: the clown and clowning are recurring images in rescuing the present by means of the past in the rest of Europe too. Meyerhold went back to the commedia in his search for images and practices to help with his break from an overtly realistic theatre. Picasso and Rouault were drawn to such imagery. In England, affection for the popular theatre is often used as a sort of moral marker, as it is by Dickens in *Hard Times* and in *David Copperfield*. Max Beerbohm wrote about Dan Leno with great admiration, T S Eliot wrote an appreciation of Marie Lloyd after her death. The images of Chaplin and Keaton have been much used. The music hall and the variety house have been often raided by the modern English theatre in its search for metaphor. The Ballets Russes found a Russian dimension in an idealisation of folk art, which Bloomsbury found far more to their taste than more home-grown theatre. There is whiff of Bloomsbury in the subsequent appreciation of the charm of such fancies, where they often stand in relation to the modern world as Romantic poetry did to Manchester in the nineteenth century. There can be something arch, too, in assumed naiveté, in identification with the commedia and clowning outside its natural environment, and in a smug English amateurism that admires a subsidised company simply for demonstrating that it is made up of good eggs.

It is to the eternal credit of Joyce and Lawrence that, of the moderns, they really didn't fall for this. It is the director-led side that has most gone for this pseudo-purity, as though other modern developments in the theatre were not chaste enough. The shade of Marie Antoinette in the Petit Trianon is moving through this correlative to the orientalism so recently castigated elsewhere, an internal colonisation to be found in celebrating the antics of the poor as medicine for the rich. Brecht is often guilty of both these class and race appropriations, which is perhaps why he struggled eventually to assert that some kind of realism is the only socialist art, and why the gauntlet thrown down by Ibsen has been very hard to pick up.

But in England there was a fetishising of the professional as a way of avoiding what the European theatre had to teach. Noël Coward's painful dictum that all an actor had to do was to remember the lines and avoid falling over the furniture was, for all its awful insight, in part what the Court theatre of George Devine was opposing: the West End shoddy that was all that was on sale.

In 1939, before the outbreak of the war which would change the social and political life of the world, Noël Coward was writing a play for the West End, which was eventually produced, with Coward playing the central character, Garry Essendine, who, like Coward, is a West End star. *Present Laughter* is the kind of play which after 1945 would be seen as increasingly foreign in a different world. The part of Essendine was tailor-made for Coward, almost bespoke, in effect a self-portrait, and the play is a puff for a world and a theatre that Coward epitomised. Essendine is at once a heterosexual lothario, and yet as camp as the proverbial row of tents. It is a part which no actor since has been able to make plausible and Paul Scofield remains the only actor I can think of who could have squared up to the improbable metro-sexuality presented. The play centres on Essendine and his demi-mondaine friends, his ex-wife, his secretary and his managers, all dependent on him for their livelihoods, all pretending to a metropolitan chic where laughs are obtained by mentioning English place names or foreign artists.

Coward's *Present Laughter* prefigures John Osborne's last notable success, *A Hotel in Amsterdam,* in which incidentally Paul Scofield played the leading part, another perhaps more believable metro-sexual type. The focus of Osborne's play is narrower than that of Coward's and concentrates on the relationship of the friends. It is more grim and real, more romantic and less funny than *Present Laughter.* Both these plays mark a point when their authors' work has become less effective as the characters they write about are increasingly less appealing, and the worlds portrayed more hermetic. They rely entirely on the writer's personality to hold the audience.

In the Coward play, the attention is more scattered, but central to it is a debate about theatrical values arising from the relationship between Essendine and a young and ridiculous interloping writer named Roland Maule. In the ensuing scenes between them, there is comic vilification of arrogant inexperience and unprofessionalism, of everything that is slapdash, pretentious, craftless and probably obscure. There is very little Shavian fair play, since Essendine/Coward is a generous, self-deprecating, English sort of a chap and the play itself, the play we are watching, is a demonstration of the values admired by Essendine, a self-congratulatory marvel set in opposition to work by Maule, which we will never see.

But theatre is a moral art, in which the spectator is free to judge for himself in a way that is difficult in the cinema, where the film-maker has greater methods of manipulation at his disposal than does the theatre director. I am reminded of a scene in a late Osborne play, *West of Suez*, in which the central character, a venal and venerated old writer, is pitted against a black woman journalist. No matter how much Osborne emphasises the failings of the compromised old charmer, there is a clear intention to show him to be a better bet than the humourless black feminist. But there was a balance to things as presented in performance which made you resolutely and equally condemn both as conniving and self serving. The theatre is a marvellous place for showing the inherent risibility in pretence that other arts seem more able to conceal, often and particularly the theatre's own pretentiousness.

What Coward is finding fun with in *Present Laughter* has proved a rich theme for English comic writers, from Gilbert and Waugh and Wodehouse down to Amis and *Private Eye*: the English fear of the pretentious and the ludicrousness of many modern artists.

It seemed as if Maugham, Lonsdale, Coward and Rattigan lived in a solipsistic metropolitan tunnel, unable – whether because of money or censorship or the status quo – to write about life as they lived it themselves,

and in mortal fear of pretence and of anything in foreign
art that wasn't French. There is in Coward a sort of instinc-
tual fear of the dangers inherent in the arty pretention
he was attacking. And indeed if it was not for men like
him and the others there would be no English theatre to
speak of. Craig and Barker, the high priests of the serious
theatre, had long before the time of *Present Laughter* left
their colleagues, as many thought, in the lurch. There was
in Coward a prescient understanding, inside what seemed
to be, and was, reactionary and self-serving, that to replace
one kind of solipsism for another would be no solution to
the theatre's needs.

At the time of writing *Present Laughter* Coward was
writing the script of David Lean's film *This Happy Breed,*
which is as patriotic and nationalist a piece of hokum
as you are likely to find outside the Soviet Union of the
time. In that year – 1939 – when Coward was writing
these and holding the West End in thrall, Meyerhold, the
great Russian animateur, was arrested by Stalin. Two years
later, when Coward produced *Blithe Spirit*, Meyerhold
was shot, his wife having already been murdered. At this
time Littlewood and MacColl and the others were in
Manchester practising a craft different to but as sophisti-
cated as Coward's, before downing tools, the men to fight
in the war during which for my generation of children,
Stalin would be turned into Uncle Joe.

Devine was a product of this compromised commercial theatre, who also took up arms in the war, in his case
in Burma, where he distinguished himself and where his

liberal politics were firmed up. He dreamed of a theatre of the kind epitomised for him by Saint-Denis and his Compagnie de Quinze in which design, directing and acting came together in one enterprise where the actor was seen as an all-round tradesman. It was liberal in politics but chiefly concerned with the art of the theatre. In practice at the Court, this vision of an art theatre collided with the more urgent needs of the writers. It was this collision of their post-war poetic concerns, the more Craigian aspirations of Devine, and the various tensions between the many voices employed, that made it such a rich and diverse theatre, where Devine risked pretension in order to free his theatre from the restrictions imposed by West End norms and made it a place where Gilbertian England was resolutely defied.

In 1959, with an irony that attends any account of the English theatre, Tony Richardson, in a raid on his old home, produced Noël Coward's adaptation of Feydeau's farce, *Occupe-toi d'Amélie* as *Look after Lulu*, which was cast up to the hilt with distinguished actors. It proved to be resoundingly dull and inexpert but, because of its star Vivien Leigh, it was also a copper-bottomed commercial success.

I met Coward once in the course of the production of his play *Waiting in the Wings* at the Olympia theatre in Dublin, when he showed the courtesy and lack of side that was typical of his generation of actors and writers that I met when young. This play concerns the trials of a group of older actresses living out their time in a retirement home and the production, by Peggy Webster, had collected together a group of distinguished older actresses, many of them long since retired themselves. They included Maureen Delaney, a veteran of the Abbey; Mary Clare, who had been the lady Tondelayo in the crowd-pleaser *White Cargo*; Norah Blaney who, with her partner Gwen Farrar, had been a successful cabaret artist; Edith Day an American musical-comedy star who had been the leading lady in the first production of *Irene* on Broadway, in which she sang 'Alice Blue Gown' and in London where she had starred in *Rose Marie and The Desert Song,* and with Paul Robeson in *Show Boat*; and other distinguished character actresses, like Nora Nicholson. The leading parts were played by Sybil Thorndike and Marie Lohr. Sybil Thorndike was, with Edith Evans, the pre-eminent actress of the time. She had created the part of Saint Joan for Bernard Shaw, had been a member of the first repertory company in Manchester, and her husband Lewis Casson was in Barker's company at the Court. She was one of the first lady actresses, the daughter of a canon of Rochester Cathedral and a much-loved and venerated figure. Marie Lohr came from more commercial theatrical stock. When young she had been a beauty and figured on the postcards of the period. She had played Lady Teazle with Tree at His Majesty's Theatre, and there used to be a portrait of her as Rostand's L'Aiglon in the Globe (now the Gielgud) theatre, which she had once managed.

I found myself in Dublin for the opening because Sophie Devine and Margaret Harris were designing it and Harris had need of company, since she was driving first to Liverpool, then going by boat to Belfast, and thence to Dublin where she and her sister were to drive to Galway after the opening. They stayed at the Shelbourne, I in Rathmines, and I used to have tea with them and the two stars sometimes. If you haven't been to tea at the Shelbourne with actresses who remember the Edwardian theatre you have missed a treat. 'I went to have my shoes mended,' Marie Lohr said to me on one such occasion. 'In the Edgware Road.' I couldn't imagine her having shoes that needed mending, or in the Edgware Road. '"Name?" said the man when I gave him my shoes. "Marie Lohr." I replied. "There used to be a very famous actress called Marie Lohr," said the cobbler. "The same."' she said, bowing to me as if to him, as women riding in landaus must have bowed when driving in Hyde Park or in the Bois de Boulogne.

When the show opened we drove out to the Dublin hills where in the course of a picnic I fell down a water-fall near Powers Court, and was fished out of the water by Harris, and awoke to find myself being given the last rites by a young priest in a hospital in Dun Laoghaire. Some days later, a card arrived from Sybil Thorndike asking if she might come and visit me, which in due course she did. As she sat next to me I could see through the window Lewis Casson, wearing a panama hat, sitting in the car they had driven out in.

There is not much of Coward's bright talent around at present, nor of Osborne's either, but there has come about a symbiosis of Essendine's mid-Atlantic, wake-up-and-smell-the-coffee, show-business orthodoxy and Roland Maule's student-drama movement-and-music one. Oh Les Beaux Jours.

●　　●　　●　　●　　●　　●

There were practical reasons, apart from purely stylistic ones, for using masks in *The Chalk Circle*. They were to do with separating out social types in a dialectic and to solve the logistics of doubling, since there were thirty of us to play some ninety parts, and most of the large number of small parts would fall to a relatively small group within the larger company. My diary begins with a description of the company's introduction to the masks which happened on the first day of rehearsals. It is contained in my first stumbling entry. The rehearsals took place principally at the Young Women's Christian Association, in the Scala theatre in Goodge Street, in the newly opened Donmar rehearsal room, and later on stage at the Aldwych theatre.

Feb 5. YMCA
It was a full company call with all the cast there except for Hugh Griffiths who isn't coming yet. Around the hall were card tables with rows of masks laid on them. Nearby, piles of clothes and walking sticks and hats. Bill Gaskill introduced us to the designer Ralph Koltai, who showed us a model of the set. It seemed to work very well. We are going to use the revolve. The play is being performed

as if by members of the collective in the prologue. The actors are going to [move] the units of scenery in the open stage, against a permanent surround. We looked at the costume designs [by Annena Stubbs] which were laid out at the back of the hall. There were about ninety of them. Then Bill Gaskill started the morning's work. We formed a playing area where the masks were and he told us about the technique we were going to use with them...

The technique is simple enough. The actor selects a mask without much study and puts it on and looks in the mirror. He must react immediately. At the beginning this is not for long. In subsequent sessions he will move away from the mirror but only when he feels can sustain the physical life that has come about almost without thought, without reflection and not by means of any traditional method of building a character. The physically expressive actor with flow and spirit will do best. Anything that resembles dance or anything that is self-conscious or worked out will fail. As a character progresses, sound appropriate to the character is produced which in turn develops into speech and eventually a sufficiently established mask moves into interaction with other masks and into conflicts that are simple and funny, driven by the peculiar obsessions that seem to motivate the characters developed by this method.

A problem soon presented itself that was inherent in the method Gaskill was using. The successful mask worked up in the studio is a sovereign creation. It is not necessarily capable of adapting to what a writer has created in a text, outside this environment, and the mask-maker's hand is in it too, so that the transfer, using this method, from rehearsal room to stage, from process to perform-ance is hard, if an existing text is used. We never satisfac-torily solved the problem. The sessions we undertook were often gruelling. And those who excelled were not always actors who were effective elsewhere, although the most talented members of the company all made a fist of it. Sue Engel, Jimmy Mellor, Patsy Byrne, Mavis Edwards, and Cherry Morris seemed the best able to access the mask easily, or are those most mentioned in this regard in the diary, though there are not many descriptions of particular improvisations described. Jimmy Bree made a particularly vivid creation recorded in one entry:

Thursday March 1. St David's day YWCA
the mask…making him [Bree] like an enormous sloppy fat child blowing raspberries and caressing his stomach, circling his finger in his own and other people's mouths… everyone at the theatre does an impersonation of him.

Later when the company was trying on masks designed for the play, there is an entry about them:

Sunday (Saturday) March 10. YWCA
Sue Engel put on a mask that was rather tragic in feeling, pale and furrowed and rather ridiculous. She was backed into a corner by Jimmy Bree, whose mask made him quick and dodgy. Sue was upset and frightened and said 'Go

Away, Go Away' and then, after he was less frightening,
'It's too late now.'

Patience Collier put on the sort of mask she is addicted
to: pretty and rather ridiculous, and pestered Cherry
Morris who was still at the mirror – she was still obviously
feeling her way in. Her not responding threw Patience,
who was more truthful in the moment. Then Cherry
turned into an insecure creature whose chief difficulty she
said was thinking. Eventually she allowed Patience to lead
her across until she stopped, too worried to move.

Mavis Edwards put on the mask Sue Engel was wearing.
Unbearable to see the long-faced creature walking a few
steps and asking, 'Can you tell me where I am? Can you
tell me who I am?'

In conjunction with this approach to character, Gaskill
introduced exercises to illustrate how he wanted us to
think as we worked on the matter of the play. In particular how we were to interpret Brecht's famous and, for
us, puzzling *verfremdungseffekt*. This is commonly translated into English as the alienation effect, giving the word
a rather harsher meaning than is intended by the German,
which suggests distancing or estrangement rather than
alienation, implying a desire to encourage the audience to
take up a critical stance towards what they are witnessing,
rather than a purely empathetic one.

This is an idea coming out of the Enlightenment, from
Voltaire in particular, an idea of shocking the audience
into a realisation of what is behind certain social gestures,

a healthy disillusion that might lead to better things. There is a continuing post-Enlightenment desire to, as it were, clean up perception, making it new, as Ezra Pound would want later. Brecht's intention was more ideological than this, demonstrating the party-political side of the Berliner Ensemble, which believed in political solutions, socialist solutions. In order to achieve this effect as far as actors were concerned, Brecht took the character work of the realistic school and married it to a more contemplative idea taken from the oriental theatre.

Stanislavski had pursued similar goals to Brecht's as far as creating a character was concerned, though this sounded anathematical at the time. His insistence on action and accurate intention and so forth prefigured Brecht by a generation. Brecht believed in the active side of this, but without the excessive use of a character's tics or an emphasis on the actor's subjective contribution to creating a character. It was this that marked the degeneration of Stanislavski's ideas in the American Method, and which encouraged performances that had a psychoanalytical dimension and narcissistic brilliance more to do with the actor's performance than the play. There is an undated note in the diary when I quote Brecht: 'This is the time when we wish we were poets to strip our slate speech clean, that out of our posture and gesture some fine thing might spring.'

Gaskill used a simple improvisation to investigate what he felt was necessary to our understanding of how we should approach the play. It proved exhausting but it was

instructive and went to the centre of what we were trying
to achieve:

Wednesday Feb 7. Scala theatre, Goodge St
Our group seems to have exhausted what work we can do
in the masks, so... Bill Gaskill asks Mavis [Edwards] for
a cigarette. She gives it. For about an hour we flounder
about trying to give complicated and emotional reasons.
Eventually we see it as a social gesture. Bill sets up an exercise involving two people. Each couple does an improvisation involving one person asking the other for a cigarette and what the result was. Afterwards the actors have
to relate to the others what had happened in the scene
they had just played. Most of us being unable to express
quite simply what in fact had happened as it would appear
to the audience, which was that A gave B a cigarette and it
was given or refused as the case might be.

The exercise was simple enough, and in the telling doesn't
sound very interesting, but Gaskill used it to great effect,
when in his best, tough, would-be Socratic manner, he
put the onus on the actor to understand, from his own
resources rather by instruction, what is being looked for.
At this time he managed to avoid the disincentive that his
method of work so often became. In various forms, this
method occupied the next stage of rehearsals, where sometimes eccentricity and chance also served their purpose, as
the next entry shows:

Thursday Feb 8. Scala theatre

Patience Collier joined our group this morning because she didn't work with either group yesterday [the company was split into groups to facilitate work]. I believe the other group is more clear-headed than us. But I think that this may be due to the fact that the director is working less in the dark [with them]. As an exercise… we had to try and explain to her what work we had done yesterday. There was the usual inability to tell what happened, but eventually we succeeded in telling what we had done. Though I don't think she really appreciated the point of why we were doing it. She then did an improvisation which she said was in Paddington Station. She was [she said] a woman waiting for her lover, who should have been at home with her family She couldn't leave the indicator board and sat next to James Bree, who had a briefcase, next to her. He took out packet of cigarettes and she asked him for one. He gave it to her.

She [Patience] was reluctant to tell the story before she did the improvisation. It was a very vivid improvisation and in the discussion afterwards we tried to see how much of her original story she had made clear.

She made most of the points but we didn't get anything out of the scene but that she was a woman in a great state. The family and child didn't come over, nor that she was waiting for her lover. That what she was waiting for was of great importance. We saw that she didn't want to move from the indicator [which would be an essential prop as would the cigarettes] and that the man was sufficiently agreeable to her to ask him for one [a cigarette] and that he was a businessman. We then did the improvisation again. Changing the man this time, Eric Flynn pretended to be a tramp. She wouldn't sit by him and moved away from the indicator and when she found she didn't have a cigarette, she didn't ask him for one, though he was smoking... Patience insisted on saying that the emotional state of the woman was the most interesting thing in the scene... The afternoon was very lively.

Collier's unreconstructed self-obsession, combined with her new-found ability to improvise, livened things up and helped our understanding. This exercise, like many of this kind, seems very simple and obvious when described but they can often, and in this case did, prove useful in getting to the heart of the matter and was marvellously effective at cutting to the business of clarity and narrative.

When the method had been established, Gaskill sought to find out how it could be applied to text as we worked on written scenes in which the company had appeared, all of them by Shakespeare. The first was from Gaskill's own production of *Richard III*, which he had done at Stratford in the last season with Edith Evans and Christopher Plummer, and in which Gordon Gostelow and Russell Hunter, who were in our company, had played the two murderers and Bill Wallis, who was also in our company, had understudied. The scene we looked at was in Act II, the scene in the tower when the murderers drown the Duke of Clarence in a butt of Malmsey.

Monday Feb 12. YWCA

Full company call. We brought our scripts this morning…
a lot of people thought we'd played enough games…and it
was time to get down to it. But now we had a new development. We worked on scenes from plays and applied
the method of finding out the story of the scene, finding
clearly where the points were made and what it was about.
To start off, Gordon Gostelow and Russell Hunter did the
scene prior to the murder of Clarence, which they played
in Bill Gaskill's production of the play at Stratford last
year. They were a little hazy on the lines at first but then
they gave a straight run-through of the scene…

Gaskill had felt that he hadn't allowed for much exploration of the scene at Stratford and that there it had been
generalised, so we began to examine it as a group, at first
with Gostelow and Hunter, and then with Bill Wallis who
had understudied them at Stratford, by using the narrative
method that we had been using only in improvisations up
until now. We were not looking for motive or interpretation but at what happened, what was the actual evidence of
the scene. We found after we had done some work that the
scene had more substance than had appeared in Gaskill's
Stratford production and that there was more to the characters than generalised portraits of low-life villainy about
to meet princely sensitivity. What they had performed at
Stratford had echoed the class bias in the society and made
it into a class bias in the production, which had relegated

these characters to a lower order of exploration than that afforded the more aristocratic ones.

This struck a note with actors who had first-hand experience of finding in, for example, film or television studios that in the lunch queue you were treated as the characters you played: those playing toffs always got served first. We found that, without special pleading or trying to make the characters more sympathetic, there were things to be discovered by even-handedness that gave the scene greater depth. We found, for example, that these unnamed men must be professional murderers for Brackenbury to have employed them and that killing was their trade no matter how they approached it. So a dimension was added to the scene, and to them and to Clarence, and this was not from textual analysis or from political bias (though the investigation may have come from that), but by an analysis of what happened in the scene on the rehearsal room floor, and that it was linked to Shakespeare's deeper intentions in the play. We found, too, on examination a comic difference between the two men, and that the comedy contrasted them with the job in hand and made the scene more disturbing, creating a difference between them and Clarence which was more real and unnerving.

My chief and only pleasant memory of *The Chalk Circle* rehearsals is of the work we did in this investigation rather than of the rehearsals it took to mount the play. I was watching something that was profoundly interesting, taking part in something that expressed the potential of working in the theatre, a demonstration of the potential of the art, independent of opinion or university chatter, an examination with actors of a scene's phenomenological nature, an empiric elucidation of the scene. Its effect on me was as profound as it was simple and remains the singular and most important and lasting thing I learned from the production, leading on from all that I had learned before and adding to it.

Working on Shakespeare in this way was revelatory, finding how the tone, the writing, were vital to any discovery of action or meaning in his plays; learning about the essential connection between the clarity required in a production of them and his purpose, instead of the muddiness and vanity of most productions of Shakespeare I had seen. It revealed also that working in translation is a difficult business.

There is something local in good theatre. My friend Michael Joyce sometimes stage-managed the World Theatre seasons at the Aldwych theatre and he remarked on the particular differences in the behaviour of the various companies he observed when they played there. The hauteur and distance of the Burgtheater, the warmth and cordiality of Ingmar Bergman's company, the grandeur and fun of the Comédie Française, the sweet courtesy of the Noh theatre company.

The difference between the English theatre and the European theatre lies partly in history. The German theatre is a modern theatre. It is essentially a court theatre and a dramaturgical theatre where things are willed, where the theatre is a tool used by an intellectual class. There is a controlling intelligence in Ibsen and Brecht that must will what is being attended to, a deciding for the audience. Shakespeare and Molière come out of the theatre, they are not writing for it. They are its creatures. They are not, like Schiller and Goethe, strangers to the art, grateful to the medium for what it offers them to use. In a Shakespeare play the writer is lost in the flow of the action and the language, the spirit is more democratic and erotic. Brecht, Ibsen and the Expressionists have no interest in expressing the flow of life as it happens and as part of the point they are making. They are essentially disengaged and suit an audience interested in finding ideas in anything that is presented.

The English theatre has an interest in realising what is happening as if it were the case. Its more empiric nature is difficult to harness to the abstract and while there has been a considerable intellectual element to it, its more intuitive and observational nature is what marks it out. The scene between the murderers and Clarence has an echo of the Mystery plays of the centuries before Shakespeare's *Richard III*.

The Mystery plays of the late medieval period, particularly those of the York and Wakefield cycles, are interesting examples of an important element in the English theatre. A vivid illustration of this is to be found in the Pinners' play in the York cycle, which dramatises the crucifixion of Christ by presenting it as a believable and contemporary event, the four soldiers charged with carrying out the crucifixion becoming, for the duration of the play, to all intents carpenters. In this they are like the Pinners, who were, in fact, nail makers and whose guild undertook its production. This may be why the action is coloured with the typical practicalities that would have occurred if the crucifixion of Christ were carried out by English craftsmen in York in the 1400s. Jesus's arms, for example, have to be pulled over pre-drilled holes that have been inexactly measured, so that his hands can fit the nailing.

The intense realism of the scene emphasises the essential corporeality of Jesus, which is at the centre of orthodox Christianity, with God becoming man, redeeming us by Christ's divine sacrifice on the cross, an idea that is so much a concern of the Catholic faith, leading to the mystical ingesting of body and blood in communion. The play creates an image of a puzzle at the centre of the Christian faith, of difference and communion between people, and between people and God in the person of Christ. In this case it is the common humanity of Jesus and the soldiers that is emphasised as well, and emphatically here, the marked difference between them. Jesus is working class, up to a point.

The chief purpose of the Mystery plays was not only to demonstrate the faith and wealth and importance of the guilds, but to show the people watching them the truth of the bible stories and to instruct them in their faith by identifying them with characters in the stories, both good and bad, in a way that was immediate, vividly and recognisably characterised. In the Pinners' play they see themselves as both the working-class torturers and the divine

Christ. This echoes a central image of the Christian story: the relationship of Jesus to the poor. In St Mark's gospel, a woman brings an alabaster flask full of precious oil to him. The disciples want to sell it and give the money to the poor. Jesus reprimands them in a seemingly anti-puritanical gibe about his short time among us and the eternal destiny of the poor. So there is always an implicit of Christ's social superiority to the very poor. The poor you will always have with you, he says – unless this is an irony of translation. It is as if poverty and the poor are structural and by implication the rich too. A bourgeois world has seen fit to take this puzzle of the difference and sameness of Christ in his relation to us as justification and divine permission for an eternal us-and-them. Even in the Christian tradition, identifying with the poor involves status.

I think that knowledge of Catholicism before the Counter-Reformation, and outside the control of a Mediterranean aristocracy, if that is possible, is useful to the understanding of the plays of the great English period since the discussion of equality is different in them to a view taken by Protestant individualism. Catholicism hangs between a profound sense of our common destiny, together with an equal acceptance of social hierarchy. But it is always concerned with the physical manifestation of God in the world, as it is in the incarnation. The word being made flesh.

The Mystery plays are a start of the modern theatre, written before the commedia dell'arte had come to its fully fashioned state. There is very little in them of the *Quem Queritis*, of the Mummers' plays, or of the Celtic dramatic rituals, the *mari llywyd*, or the similar rituals in Ireland, except that they share something of the celebratory aspect of these, and unlike say, Mozart's Mass in C minor, they are religious but not liturgical. I was interested then to find out the difference and the synthesis of these things European and native, old and new.

We did work similar to that which we did on *Richard III* on other scenes of Shakespeare in which members of the company had been, but not on plays in the current rep. I can remember wishing we could have done a scene from *As You Like It*, in which I was playing, but we didn't out of proper feeling. The diary tells of two other scenes, but only one of the entries records what we discovered. The diary of that day continues:

> We did some of the induction scene from *The Taming of the Shrew,* in which Mavis Edwards and Roy Dotrice had played the Hostess and Christopher Sly, and after this David Buck and Gordon Gostelow played Conrade and Borachio from *Much Ado About Nothing*. They were terribly funny and we rolled about...

Yet when we began to discus what Gostelow and Buck had conveyed to us, we couldn't say. The section of the scene in question is the one where, overheard by the Watch, Conrade tells Borachio, how he has wooed Margaret,

Hero's gentlewoman, in Hero's place at her window, and how Claudio, Don Pedro and Don John, having witnessed this, mistaking Margaret for Hero, and thinking that Hero has broken faith with Claudio, disgrace her. As an adjunct to this scene, the Watch, overhearing Conrade and Borachio and stumbling on the truth, are able to clear her good name. It is a scene vital to understanding the plot and it is in fact the *nothing* about which there is *much ado*. Shakespeare, recognising the implausibility of the plot, dramatises it by means of report, Conrade telling Borachio what has happened.

In the production in question however, there was an inserted dumb show, with the actress playing Margaret dressed as Hero leaning out of the widow. This was aiming at clarity another way and in so doing gave our actors licence to concentrate on the comedy of the scene, rather than on its part in the narrative, which they understood to have been made clear elsewhere. Much of the scene is expressed in elaborate and obscure word play, which Buck and Gostelow much relished and, as actors before actors, made us laugh heartily. This interpretation gave Gaskill good material so that we could work on the scene to make it function as Shakespeare must have intended. The use of two ideas – the psychological and the narrative – may have been alien to Shakespeare but there is enough in his Christian materialism to make them useful rather than whimsical tools.

This invention, based on the improvisations of the giving and taking of a cigarette, admirably fitted Gaskill's purpose of investigating Brecht's intentions. We used the ideas coming out of the improvisations as an approach to all the scenes when we began to rehearse the play, but early on things were lost sight of. As the production developed, with the mundane norms of conventional rehearsing imposing themselves, things became dull and routine, much to the relief of many in the company, but not before Gaskill made a proposal which typifies some of the production's aspirations and some of its eccentricity. This is recorded in the only entry in the diary worth printing in full. I had taught myself to type from a book and I had bought an Olivetti typewriter, all to help solve the problem of my unusually poor handwriting, but the tabulation defeated me and I think this was the last thing I typed until I recently conquered the computer:

Tuesday Feb 13. Scala Theatre
Full Company call…

…Bill Gaskill tells us that he has a problem which under ordinary circumstances he would have to cope with himself, but which because the work so far has involved all of us so much he thinks we should discuss collectively. He has to get a complete cast list ready for the costumiers and as most of us have been contracted to play only one part, the casting of us in the remainder has been rather arbitrary. He wants us to decide whether or not we should extend our work so far to include ignoring our contracts and deciding as a group which actor should play what parts.

In the discussions that follow there is a general feeling that the idea is a good one but that in the circumstances it is impracticable. We have five weeks left in which to rehearse the play. This will only be long enough to actually work on the text. If the company is first to cast itself and then to work on with the director in the manner that we have been doing so far – deciding whether or not what the actor is doing is actually what is required in the play – we would need more time and the problems that will crop up will be too difficult to cope with. We have signed contracts with the management – are they going to accept our tearing of them up? Do all the actors want to give up their parts? It is the director's job to cast the play before rehearsals begin, some people say. It is not the actor's responsibility. Actors like to be told what to do, to be instructed.

The discussion becomes impassioned. People split into groups and have to be asked to make what they are saying heard. Reasonable argument is being replaced by heated speeches. 'Look,' says the stage-management, 'the costumes have to be made for the first night. This way they will never be.' 'The actors are more important then the costumes,' says the director. 'First nights have been postponed before this.' 'Our responsibility is to the public,' says Keith Green, the stage director, 'and on the 29th our job is to give a cracking good show.' Some of us laugh.

I find myself speaking amongst the loudest. Since everything is becoming muddled and unreasonable one sees that people who were prepared to argue sensibly, are under fire of rash phrases, becoming afraid of the initial suggestion. Some people, seeing that the director has not yet got the problems of directing this cast in the play cut and dried, obviously distrust his ability to cope with situations that would arise. All of us are moved by the situation to state our ordinary personal values more emphatically. Why has the situation become so hot and miserable?

Issues about our lives as actors outside this production are being discussed. We belong to a profession full of people who commonly suffer from material insecurity. We belong to the Royal Shakespeare Company. Some of us have three-year contracts. We do not want to jeopardise what security we have in coping with some scheme we are not sure of. We want to be artists, but we want to be artists without taking too many risks. Our environment in the theatre has led us to this position where we wish to negate any responsibility which involves change. The contradictions of a company which on the one hand does *The Devils*, *Becket* and *Ondine*, and on the other gives marvellous conditions of staging rehearsals and stage management to a play like *The Caucasian Chalk Circle*, are mirrored in the oscillations of thinking that goes on in the discussion.

A lot of green-room bitterness about the company comes out. People see their position in the hierarchy in danger. The whole thing proposed knocks at the tradition of not talking about your money to other artists. People would have to discuss whether A's contribution to the work merited his being paid a larger salary than B. Also of course some people are insecure about their abilities. They feel they may be landed with lesser parts if the most suitable actor for the role is cast in it. The rights of the individual are of course emphasised. Some people say that the discussion of one actor's interpretation should be between the director and himself and that forty actors saying you were wrong was not necessarily true. Keith Johnstone, the director's assistant, makes the point that what has been proposed does not involve a democratic count of heads in which the majority holds the power, but depends on us deciding and thinking reasonably as a group.

Nothing is resolved. We end the discussion with most of us worried as to how rehearsals are going to go after this. It has been like a massive improvisation for the prologue to the play. In the play two collectives dispute over which of them should have a particular valley. The Galinsk farmers claim the right of ownership to a piece of land they consider home. The Rosa Luxembourg collective claims the valley for a scheme that will make their own land and this more fruitful. Both collectives agree finally that the valley should go to the Rosa Luxembourg farmers as they will make the most use of it. We differ largely from the farmers in the prologue in that while like them, most of us express our views in emotional terms, a large section of our opinion accepts the idea of how we should work but is unable to suggest any way of implementing it. Our basic difference, however, is that while they all share the same convictions we certainly do not. And it is this variation in our values that makes the way of working discussed look so impossible.

The history of the theatre is full of anecdotes designed to deflate reputations and to keep feet on the ground, as much as to bear witness to the truth, and since only the playwright produces anything that can be judged objectively *post hoc*, these stories can help bring a sense of reality to the golden ageism that so often colours the narrative and can be helpful to the young, who are often overwhelmed by the mythologising. If you think, for example, that the current critical assessment of actors and directors is in some cases wide of the mark, it can lead you to a healthy scepticism of the assessment of actors and directors in the past. But anecdotes that are evidence of the frailty of apparent gods are often no more than *schadenfreude* too, and grist to a reactionary mill.

There is a certain amount of glee to be obtained for some when they are told that Craig's set for Stanislavski's production of *Hamlet* was incapable of being built, or when it is remembered that Helene Weigel, Brecht's last wife and the artistic director of the Berliner Ensemble, suggested that the *verfremdungseffekt* was no more than Brecht's way of preventing over-acting. Actors writing or remembering can only chronicle what it felt like to be part of the process of a production and what their feeling was of being in it, not what it was like to experience the work when finished. There are endless stories of actors and dancers being in productions much loved by others which *they* thought were bogus or hateful. These are part of the story, and histories of all kinds are often qualified or trimmed according to the time and new evidence, when they are revisited.

My friend Gillian Barge occasionally wrote to me in the last months of her life and in one of her letters talks about being in Seneca's *Oedipus*, translated by Ted Hughes and directed by Peter Brook for the National Theatre at the Old Vic. Actors have stories like sailors do. Here is one:

> I was young, about twenty-seven…and was thrilled to find myself in the Old Vic working with Laurence Olivier and beginning to be given good parts from time to time. I think I had been there under a year when we heard that Peter Brook was coming to do a production… The first thing I remember learning about Peter was that he hadn't wanted to use members of the company in his production, we were insufficient in some way, but Olivier insisted he did… There was a Saturday morning rehearsal that I was never asked to attend… The rehearsals were about lying on the floor and only making a sound if it came from the depth of your being… I was really going for it, my commitment was totally in there, although I thought that, though Irene Worth was a wonderful actress, some of the things she did that Peter thought were wonderful were to my mind a bit silly. And then came the day when we were split up into groups of about six, given verses of the Chorus, and sent to a dressing room where we worked on our own for a week. Our task was to render the verse

into sounds only, and not a sound was to be decided on unless it came from the depths of our soul's being and heart... It was crushingly hard and upsetting work; we tore ourselves apart trying to achieve the truth Peter had asked of us. At the end of the week we recorded our efforts and Peter was to listen to it. I was terribly shocked on the Monday morning to find that Peter and Richard Peaslee had orchestrated the tapes, taken what they found useful, discarded what they didn't like, and gave us various sounds/noises to be made on various words or sentences... I don't think I was naïve enough to think you could only express pure truth on the stage, and I don't think would have objected to our being orchestrated, but I would have liked to have been a participant in the process and not to be manipulated into giving the production what was needed almost by mistake.

And that was what I felt about Peter's direction in the end. He didn't want to work with us, he wanted to trick and manipulate us into giving him what he wanted... I remember getting into a real crisis... I would have to leave, but that would have meant sacrificing my precious place in Olivier's company at the Old Vic, so I decided to cheat. It was the only thing I could think of, and so I was there only in body. Peter noticed of course and I probably just confirmed his prejudice about English actors, Had I been older and wiser I would have spoken to him but I was shy and frightened of authority in those days.

The performance I saw of Peter Brook's production of Ted Hughes' adaptation of the Seneca *Oedipus* bore very little evidence of what Barge and other actors felt about being in it. It was a committed and stylish production, typically chic and exhilarating. There are many stories about directors which seek to set the record – if not straight then less certain, stories that give the lie to bullshit. Bulgakov tried to blow the whistle on Stanislavski in his novel *Black Snow*, and there many stories about Brook that try to emphasise the show-business element of his work that many perceive as underpinning its apparent seriousness. That it is in some ways fake. All good directors need actors with temperaments suited to them. Barge was an idealist who needed to know whether she was storming the barricades or pretending to storm them.

Different methods of work suit different people. Many a working actor learns to fake it, in productions with a process that doesn't really suit them, or to make out as best they can, managing to be on board while keeping their counsel; or they are realistic about expectation and more sophisticated about playing the rules of particular games. Barge later found a home with the Joint Stock Company, where the democratic attempt suited her, and where at least she felt that the playing field was an even one and found herself able to accommodate to a democracy which nevertheless still depended on the dominance of directors like Gaskill and Stafford-Clark. In another letter, Barge recalls working with John Dexter:

The first time I worked with John Dexter was in a production of *A Woman Killed with Kindness* as the Old Vic… He was always on my side, from then on, and he always cast me whenever he could. John's reputation came before him, so all the actors were scared stiff before they even started rehearsal, due to the stories of his fierceness and his habit of having whipping boys. The stories are correct by the way. I was cast as the lady JP in *Equus*, the first production of Peter Shaffer's new play.

John Dexter had directed Peter's previous play *The Royal Hunt of the Sun*. It had been hugely successful and for many people had been the most wonderful and moving experience they had in the theatre. This was true for me, and Clive [Merrison] says he saw it five times. It was only on the fifth time of seeing it and hearing it he started to have considerations about the dialogue. Most of the young actors in the company at that time had been in *The Royal Hunt of The Sun* and hated it, not only because they had to black-up for each performance but because they thought the writing was laughable. They used to quote it to me and I must say that it did sound a bit daft. So we came to *Equus*. I read it. It was long and rambling and I didn't get much sense of the play. John talked about the play on the first day of rehearsal; I can't remember what he said apart from the task he gave us overnight. We were to go home and read the play and come back the next morning with some insight into our character or maybe some other aspect of the play. I went home and read it and lo, I had an insight into my character which excited me so much that when I was standing in the queue in the canteen next to Peter Shaffer I told him just what this marvellous insight was. I can still remember exactly where we were standing in the canteen in the bowels of the theatre. How can I ever forget? But then I was young... ish. 'Oh Peter,' I said, 'I realised when I read the play last night that of course my character isn't a real character but a kind of mouthpiece for information that people need to know,' or something along those lines. Peter looked completely crestfallen and muttered 'Well, I don't like writing characters that aren't real you know.' Our relationship never really recovered...

It was what I call a cardigan part; no personality, no background. I had been right in my overnight insight. However, John Dexter was directing, so any doubts about the play were eradicated by the fire of his vision. He approached the play as if it was holy writ. Everything was hugely meaningful, every actor had to be there all day and every day. The set was a square ring; all the moves had to be in straight lines. If you were not in the scene, you sat in a chair just outside the square. It was as if the play could not come into existence other than by everybody's full attention, every moment of the rehearsal day. It was mind-bogglingly boring but he was creating something and, although he was indeed frightening and did have his whipping boys, the fact was he was an artist of great genius. I think we all of us saw what was happening and admired him tremendously.

Meanwhile however I was having great trouble in my cardigan. I was taken to have supper with Helena Kennedy, as Peter said my character was based on her, but I felt frustrated from the meeting because I didn't have her dialogue. I remember John shouting at me, 'I want you to dominate this scene,' and I wanted to shout back, 'How can I with dialogue like this?' But Peter S was there, and I couldn't. I had to turn to the failsafe of all young girls and burst into tears.

Of course everyone knew what a success the show was. People stood and cheered. It was again the theatrical experience of their lives. They cried, they laughed. I always hated it. But did John know? I think he did all that holy writ stuff to control the actors.

Now Barge always had a problem with authority and she didn't have the nous of actors who appear to be onside and yet who do not take a director more seriously than suits them. Of course, part of her admiration for Dexter was because of his enthusiasm for her, and her fear of Brook was linked to the fact that she and the other youngsters in the Vic company felt that he didn't really want them to be in the production. It's a question of whose seriousness you are happy with, but the tone of a production is usually set by the director and the experience of being part of a production is very different from the experience of those watching it. I can, with the help of my diary, recall much of the rehearsals of the *Chalk Circle* but nothing at all of the performance we gave.

After the discussion that seemed to be about the nature of democracy, rehearsal took an almost determinist conventional route as if that discussion, while it demon-strated in its way much of what Brecht is talking about in the play, had marked the end of the investigation of it. I can't imagine discussions like it were the order of the day at the Berliner Ensemble, or anywhere in East Germany at the time, where the theatre was more hierarchical than ours. By their nature there are always restrictions to the aspirations of rehearsals, but Gaskill failed to manage with enough skill even the generous amount of time that we had, in relation to other rehearsal periods. It seemed to me that the idea of the play was more interesting to him than its execution, but the rehearsals were not without incident, as ordinary silliness became part of the process, and this entry shows two ways of looking at the theatre coming into conflict:

Saturday February 17
We worked on the section of the play called 'The Noble Child' on Friday. In the afternoon Bill Gaskill was working with Michael Flanders, who is playing the narrator, so Keith Johnstone took the rehearsal. Patience Collier voted

not to talk about the scene but to discuss the character of the Governor's wife. Keith made the point that...at the moment, the exercise was to tell the story and make clear to ourselves what was going on...we weren't sure what the political situation [was] in Grasina, which was important for the [story – Patience was to play the wife of the Governor of the town –] and if we don't understand it, the audience never will. Patience said she didn't want to do this but to talk about her character. The atmosphere got tiresome; there was a row ostensibly about our work but in which Russell Hunter got at Patience. She left and we got on with the scene. Rehearsals are going on more ordinarily now. People are tired of talking and want to work. The week has been extremely dull.

I can't remember this encounter between Johnstone and Collier but it illustrates the quite different ways of thinking about the theatre that were present then. Patience Collier was an experienced if limited actress who would at first sight be seen to be born out of the conventional West End theatre. In fact, her beginnings were in Manchester, where she had worked with Joan Littlewood. She became one of the nucleus of actors at the centre of the RSC. She was rather chic in her way, one of those actresses who hates their own hair, so she always wore turbans or scarves wound round her head. Unusually plain, and yet with style in the Helena Rubinstein way. She delighted in being trouble and was indulged in this delight at the RSC. She was more tiresome than really difficult, and very loyal to Hall, who was very loyal to her.

Johnstone and she were as opposite as you could get. Keith had a heavy post-war look with his thick spectacles and sweater and slacks like a character in John Braine or Colin Wilson. He had absolutely no enthusiasm, or feeling for, or knowledge of the conventional theatre of the day, having come from teaching as a would-be playwright. He had very little talent for directing in any practised sense of the word and consequently his productions were usually disastrous, but he was very interested in the mechanics of performing. His was a typical variant of Devine's Court. He had little in common with Anderson or Richardson or Dexter but he found an ally in Gaskill, who had directed a short play of his, and he became a successful, enlightened and even-handed literary manager at the Court, the first in Britain.

The writers group he and Gaskill ran in the Hammersmith drawing room of one of the Court's early writers, Ann Piper, included Edward Bond, Ann Jellicoe, and John Arden, all of whom produced work influenced by those meetings. Later Johnstone and Gaskill ran an everyone-is-welcome comedy workshop for actors at the Jeannette Cochrane Theatre, which I helped to organise, and which marked the start of the work that Johnstone put down later in his book *Impro* which had such an effect on the teaching of drama in universities, and on some of the improvisatory stand-up comedy that was to come later, just as Gaskill's other collaborator, N F Simpson, had had an impact on the surreal comedy on television that came after him. But it wasn't the comic side of Johnstone's work that interested me. It was the physical and visual images that he and his actors in Theatre Machine, the company he developed later, created – rough, underground, rather art-school, almost childish images, writer-created images, rather than ones drawn from directorial fancy.

I learned in those classes, and in the *Chalk Circle* rehearsals, how different being a talented studio actor could be, as opposed to being an actor in plays in the more democratic world of paid performance. I also learnt from this work that, while directing needs some internal creative impulse, there is a phenomenological element to a play that requires addressing; there can be a piety attending process as a must, that is no different in its tyranny from the pieties of over-professionalisation. And that both are an enemy of the serious theatre.

I don't think Gaskill really accepted, or faced the grind involved in dealing with Brecht's play. Brecht needs a greater sense of the material world than Gaskill gave it and it wasn't until I read the diary that I realised that Michael Flanders and Hugh Griffiths, the two heavyweights in the production, were not included in much of what the rest of us did, though the diary includes some admiring references to Griffiths. As for Collier's interventions, they were at least upfront and manageable, not so the undercurrent of sourness I felt had become institutionalised in the RSC. Beyond that, the diary entries largely tell the story of routine and increasingly unsatisfying rehearsals. There are some inconsequential entries:

19 February. Donmar rehearsal room
This big rehearsal space, which Donald Albery has built. It has as much equipment for you to dress rehearse and light some plays…has a machine which sells horrid coffee. Plotted the noble child.

There are some entries about Hugh Griffiths, but not many:

February 20
…Hugh Griffiths who is going to play Asdak joined us today. Astonished to see how much less extraordinary he is. We read the second half of the play [the story of the judge]. How well he phrased. Wasted a lot of the time arguing about changing odd words. I was glad to see that he was suited to the part. I thought that he was more actorish than he appears. Wasted most of the afternoon arguing about the translation.

Wednesday February 28. YMCA
We did the Fat Duke Scene today… See how Hugh Griffiths actually feels the quality of what he's speaking. You can…see him physically explore his way into the part.

The diaries occasionally mention something not concerned with the production. I had recently landed a tiny part in a film about a mutiny on board a Royal Navy ship during the Napoleonic Wars:

Theatre Feb 22
Was Driven home by Michael Flanders. Saw stills of *HMS Defiant*.

But the entries become more and more laconic as the rehearsals follow a conventional route.

Saturday February 24. YMCA
Wedding scene. Seem to have given up on the democratic idea. I'm sorry.

There are two more interesting entries about now, concerning two of the great actresses of the day: Peggy Ashcroft and Edith Evans. Ashcroft was almost a fixture at Stratford-upon-Avon during the artistic directorship of Glen Byam Shaw. She had been associated with many of the interesting developments in the theatre of her time, and she was a favourite with many of the most important actors and directors. Her qualities always remained those of an attractive *ingénue*, but she was a brave and committed actress, her politics having been firmed up when she received abuse as a young actress for playing Desdemona opposite Paul Robeson. She had worked with Gielgud and Komisarjevsky and Saint-Denis, in whose production of

The Cherry Orchard she was currently playing Ranyevskaya for the RSC. She was an old friend of George Devine and was on the board of the Royal Court Theatre, where she had played Rebecca West in *Rosmersholm*, and had been in a production of *The Good Person of Setzuan* playing the good woman Shen Te and the wicked man Shiu Ta.

> *Monday February 26*
> In the break between the matinee and evening show, an announcement over the tannoy of *The Cherry Orchard* asking those concerned with *The Chalk Circle* to go to the green room. There they waited...until suddenly the door slammed open and in came a masked man, pouring out invective, pushing the women against the wall. They didn't know who it was and imagined it was some Bill Gaskill stunt about mask work, when the figure took off the mask and there was Peggy Ashcroft who had been wearing the Shiu Ta mask from the production of *The Good Woman of Setzuan* at the Royal Court.

And not long after the note about Ashcroft's demonstration of fellowship, there is one about Edith Evans, the supreme actress of the age. She was never as adventurous and committed as Ashcroft and Thorndike, but she was an outstanding actress, a rare one. She and the poet Christopher Hassall gave a recital of poetry interlaced with scenes from some of the plays she had been in, which made for an opportunity to see and hear her playing some of the parts for which she had been famous. It remains for me one of the most important and informing evenings in the theatre I have ever had.

March 4

Last night there was an Apollo Society recital on the stage of the Aldwych. It would have been one of those tiresome cultural evenings but our greatest actor Edith Evans was performing... Watching the superb playing of the wooing scene in *As You Like It*, what I was struck by most was that she absolutely perceives the nature of the character... And the nature of the scene... She played this at immense speed...setting in your ears the timing and sense of the line on the page. It is fascinating to see her doing for Shakespeare what we would like to do for Brecht. I suppose you would describe style as how you convey what the scene is about. Given that you are talented and reasonably equipped, seek to express truthfully what the nature of the person is and character should lead you to be what is known as very stylish.

There was in this recital a marvellous synchronicity with our rehearsals, since it demonstrated to me something we had been searching for and which was so simple and so hard to do. This seemed to me to be not much more than to find out what you are actually doing, and then find out how to do it. *What* and *how* being the key words, with *why* kept as a reserve, since it is not the practical word. This seemed to me then what Brecht and Evans, Stanislavski and Barker had aimed to do; they made a proposition which gave the challenge to my generation of what do to next. I think this is what made the next section of rehearsal seem so inexorably dull and frustrating, as these entries will tell, though things are not made any better by the standard of the writing:

Thursday March 1. St David's Day YMCA
...The rehearsal wasn't a very inspiring one. The initial exercises we did seem a long way off. I wonder if they made any difference... to the work. It's hard to tell. The day of the famous discussion has had no effect. We are rehearsing the play as normal ...

Saturday March 3
...A lot of the company seem to think things are dull and we have done too much talking. Difficulty with the translation. Susan Engel gets it in German, explains it to us word by word.

March. YMCA
...We need some sort of jollying up rehearsal...until we get to the technical.

Sometimes the diary suggests light at the end of the tunnel, particularly as we begin to use the stage and the attendant excitement that this can bring. The technical rehearsals mark a curious period for an actor, both exciting and enervating, as he is only peripheral to what's going on. The entries after this veer between an increasing sense of

frustration, together with a straw-catching sense of possibility. I think it marks the unacknowledged frustration of
a young actor with too many small parts. Griffiths and
Byrne and Dotrice might have had a quite different experience than mine. I think too that Brecht is not a particularly nourishing writer to rehearse and Gaskill is not one
to feel he has to make up the deficit in any way at all.

Wednesday March 7. Aldwych Theatre
…first rehearsal on stage …wasn't a full stage as, with the
As You Like It set in the dock, a lot of *The Cherry Orchard*
stuff has to be stacked at the back of the stage and piled
in the wings… One of the difficulties Jimmy Mellor and
I have is being aristocratic enough… We're more used to
being matey with people than saying 'Off with his head'.
We rely greatly on others. Bill said when he was rehearsing Edith Evans as Margaret in *Richard III* at Stratford
she said it was all right pretending she was regal quietly to
herself but she was done for if the others didn't behave as
if they thought she was.

Thursday March 8. YWCA
It really is too bad that the time hasn't been used more
economically.

Friday March 9. YWCA
…A section of the company thinks that rehearsals are
going very badly… I think what makes the task so difficult… is our inability… to relate on stage. I suppose it is an
English actor's characteristic to be in a little well-rehearsed

vacuum, presenting a performance that is the result of his personality meeting the character. We miss at the moment a communal vitality...the company's performance of *The Cherry Orchard* lack of emotional generosity one actor to another as it appeared to me. Made nonsense of the play...

And later in the same entry:

Only two or three of the characters go through the play and develop...

For them it is like rehearsing a part in another play. When you're rehearsing a play your part usually goes through it. If you're rehearsing act one, what you find out about the character helps you play the whole play. Here, it's like rehearsing a lot of plays and so the development is slow and everything seems under rehearsed... you have no time to develop. That is why Brecht needs the physical reality.

And in this state of increasing dissatisfaction and unhappiness the diary goes into the last stage of the rehearsals where things swing between good and mostly bad:

Saturday March 10. YWCA
We put on some of the masks designed for the play... enormous leap forward... In spite of the fabulous morning's work, I didn't think the company was in a much better state. This afternoon we had a run-thro of the whole play.

It was rather a gruesome experience. First of all there were a lot of people from the organisation there, Peter Hall and Michel Saint-Denis… We had Dudley Moore to accompany us on the piano. Roy Dotrice has had a car accident and is in hospital so Simon Chachava was read by the stage management and Russell Hunter, who understudies him as Firs and some other people, had to go and rehearse for tonight's performance [of *The Cherry Orchard*]. The play is very long and the afternoon was very exhausting.

Sunday March 17. Aldwych
Today we had a dress parade. It was a very satisfying morning because everybody loved the clothes; they have been very carefully and skilfully made. There must have been about 60 costumes. All the masks were there. Some, most, are to be made more comfortable. Rehearse the wedding. We did a lot of work… worries that we will be compared to the Berliner…

Then on stage where I experienced, as I used to when young, a feeling of transport that can come when a production makes its way from the rehearsal room and onto the stage, when all the elements that go up to making a performance, all the different skills come together and produce unrehearsed images, chance ones created as problems are solved, inconsequent images, as when the stage boys stand while something is sorted, always seeming to catch a perfect light and standing in undirected groups as if in a great picture. The time when people come, as it were, from different tribes and gather in the theatre to play out one of Western civilisation's most ancient rituals: the useless business of putting on a play:

March 13. Aldwych theatre
…This section of the rehearsal period is for me very like a drug. On the stage, groups of actors tried on their masks and worked quietly in twos. Some showed what they were doing to us watching in the stalls, the white light cast shadows… like that time sometimes at a working weekend in the theatre, when everything is very quiet and the stage management are there, in the night time, and actors are coping with door handles and curtain runners. The first night seemed a date we would arrive at in our own time, and reviews and bar bells and black ties were remote and didn't matter.

Wednesday March 21
Run-through. Seemed in good shape we had all the masks… (some) of us … were using the mask for the first time … playing without… the intermediate work…

Friday March 23
Today we go through part one… Music director complaining music not ready …Ralph Koltai flippant boring manner…

Saturday March 24 Afternoon. YWCA
Dance rehearsal. Worked more on the final dance. Litz Pisk annoyed because Dudley hasn't written the music

and she thinks we'll get used to the rehearsal tune. The non-dancers were rehearsing in the theatre.

Litz Pisk was a tiny dark-haired Viennese woman, mostly to be seen with her practice skirt tucked up into her waistband, one of those gifts of the Nazis who benefited the theatre here, during and after the war. She had taught at the Old Vic School and was at the time head of movement at Central School, where she was much respected. She and other teachers produced by the European modern dance movement were a great influence here, principally through three teachers: Pisk in London; Rudolph Shelley, who was a great influence at the Bristol Old Vic school, where he brought an understanding particularly of gifted students; and, perhaps most notably and influentially, Rudolph Laban, who had been promoted by the Nazis until he fell foul of them and was forced to flee. His theory of the psychological element implicit in movement had great influence here and was an influence on the training programme that the early Theatre Workshop-pers devised for themselves, when he worked with them in person. He was an inveterate Expressionist, as was Yat Malmgren, who taught a version of his system and was an influence at the Court, through Gaskill's enthusiasm for him, and at the Drama Centre, the school he co-founded.

Dudley Moore was known then principally as a composer and jazz musician. His fame was still to come. The great success of the university revue *Beyond the Fringe* had not yet projected him into a career that would end in

Hollywood. He had been at Oxford with Anthony Page and had, through him, worked at the Court, which is where the connection with this production was made.

March 25
Technical of Act 2. Things seemed a little better today... The play has been lit after a fashion. I like the look of the scenery more. The copper screen is a marvellous colour... At 8 o'clock we began a no-stopping dress rehearsal without music. We got through well... I think the fact of having gone through it made everyone feel better...

Notes took until 2 o'clock. The oddest general one was that we shouldn't hurry things.

Monday March 26 2 o'clock Afternoon
By the time we got to the dress rehearsal, this time with orchestra, we had no time to put things right that had gone wrong yesterday, no time to practise things that we decide to change in notes... the fluke of the technical being right yesterday... combined with... the actors having in some way risen to the occasion. The rehearsal was by comparison a bit of a fiasco.

Tuesday March 27 12 o'clock
Notes from Bill in the stalls. John Roberts, manager, and Peter Hall sitting at the back. The notes were rather lackadaisical and Bill transmitted a sort of helplessness disguised as objectivity. He said that it had gone very badly the night before and that what we did lacked interest and clarity. He said that we would work the flight to the mountains

and the Noble Child and then dress rehearse. Second half better, but very down.

This begins a very scanty record of the rehearsals, during which I remember feeling utter misery:

2 o'clock
Bill called us on stage and said that Peter Hall felt he hadn't stressed the gravity of the situation enough and that he was going to take the rehearsal today. Peter Hall stressed that he didn't disagree with the production, just that it needed tightening up.

I was a friend of Gaskill's, so I hid my disappointment with him and my resentment of Hall in a cloak of hurt Celtic loyalty to Gaskill, but I kept my head down as best I could and worked hard.

There were three allegiances in the subsidised theatre in London at the time. Loyalties which had become, for some people, political and almost religious, and were partial in the way only sects broadly in one religion can be. The Court theatre and Stratford East were in opposition to the RSC. Court apparatchiks admired the work at Stratford East, Stratford East did not admire the Court. The RSC, having the greater resources, was able to poach successfully from the other two. My own allegiance was to the Court, which was not so much a one-man band as was Stratford East, where I admired all the productions but not the culture which seemed based on old-fashioned

Communism, infiltrated by chic Soho anti-establishment-ism, together with a taste for glorifying criminals. To some insiders at Stratford East it seemed to be a sell-out of the original aims of the company. To others, the work there was the epitome of all that had been good before but in a more realised and achieved way.

I never saw a production there that I did not admire. It seemed to me the work of a collaboration of a singular kind, even if centred on one person, which is perhaps why the plays they did have not for the most part survived. Littlewood was a London girl of unprivileged back-ground who went to RADA and left there to hitch-hike to Manchester to take up a job in BBC radio. She had been a friend of Frith Banbury and Stephen Haggard at RADA. In Manchester, she met Ewan MacColl, who is perhaps the originator of the work we all associate with her. He it was who recognised her obvious directorial talent. They relied on the commitment of a group of actors – amateur ones, of whom Howard Goorney was with her until the end. In the course of the work, she met two other remark-able men: Gerry Raffles, who was a gifted enabler, and John Bury, whose talent as a designer grew in part out of the conditions of work, part out of necessity. By the time I saw the productions, MacColl had long since parted company with Littlewood. All the productions I saw of hers had enormous *joie de vivre,* energy and style, and one after another of them were glorious things. Gerry Raffles was the perfect manager for her.

At Devine's theatre, life was being analysed in less of a cartoon way, though often with less vim, and I thought it was more serious and less exclusive. The Court and Stratford East suffered from the lack of enough government support, so that eventually Littlewood, by now without the support of Raffles, who had died prematurely, and John Bury who had gone to the RSC, found herself in an increasingly alienated situation. She lacked the stability to fulfil schemes – like the fun palace she talked of – which were difficult to realise, certainly by her alone. Her eventual retirement, to a house in France on the estate of one of the Rothschilds, was a great loss and a great surprise. She had succumbed to commercial pressures which marked a sad end to an enterprise as heroic and courageous as anything undertaken in the modern theatre. The production of *Twang*, a musical about Robin Hood which she eventually disowned, put me off any taste for fake populism for life.

At the RSC there seemed to be a structural compromise, which my younger self could not bear. There is nothing in the diaries about Hall's rehearsals, which I think did the necessary job of getting the show into an acceptable length. The diary continues sometimes in a gnomic way:

The whole of today had a wonderful complexity to it... One's own *Middlemarch* taking place.

There is very little about Hall's intervention and the diary ends by tailing off:

Wednesday March 28

12 o'clock ... Dress rehearsal; some of the public in. Went very well. We put the pace on. Music and songs worked better and scene changes and getting on and off, and the pressure having been put on bore results. Afterwards had notes. Could see the point of having a fresh face to look at it. Notes finished at 2 o'clock.

Thursday March 29

Still no Bill. Notes from Peter Hall...Worked on the wedding scene... worked one scene change... Worked on Jussup.

In the afternoon decided whether or not to cut the blackmailer scene. 7 o'clock, first performance.

And that entry ends my diary of *The Chalk Circle* rehearsals. There is no indication after it of how the first night went or how the play and the production were received. In fact, the press and public reception was good and, for most of the company, once the pressure of the last days was off, it turned into a show like any other, and most of them had had worse experiences. But I can remember David Buck – with whom, together with some others of the company, I shared a dressing room – being furious and showing it on the press night, when the show seemed to be going well, which is a measure of some of the sourness of that company and what I so disliked about it. But actors like Patsy Byrne and Hugh Griffiths were too talented, too experienced, and too suited to their parts for a performance of *The Chalk Circle* with them leading a talented company to be poor. With a characteristic eccentricity Gaskill had gathered on side collaborators that included Keith Johnstone, Dudley Moore, Ralph Koltai, Litz Pisk, Annena Stubbs, Robert Ornbo, and Michael Flanders, who were too interesting and too talented for the performance to be dud.

●   ●   ●   ●   ●   ●

It was in the next season for the RSC at Stratford that Gaskill showed to great effect what he had learned and had been investigating in *The Chalk Circle,* when he directed *Cymbeline.* It remains one of the best achieved and most exhilarating Shakespeare productions I have ever seen. Vanessa Redgrave played Imogen and some of the *Chalk Circle* company, including Patience Collier, were in it. The design was by René Allio, who had worked extensively with Roger Planchon with the TNP at Lyon on productions of both Shakespeare and Brecht, and who was very much in tune with what Gaskill wanted. The understanding of narrative and how to achieve it that Gaskill had examined in *The Chalk Circle* seemed to have paid off. It had none of the nervousness or posing or laziness of the Brecht production and, with an added feeling for the writing, it struck the balance between romance and tragedy with extraordinary insight and clarity. Clarity is sometimes thought to be anaemic or worthy. That production had an almost voluptuous clarity and speed that was unusual and astounding.

Gaskill is a situationist as much as he is a director and a sort of refusenik for a very variable creed. I remember around the time of the diary going to a class or talk he was giving at the City Literary Institute, where he sat on the teacher's rostrum and didn't say a word until the class got restive and embarrassed and of course angry. I don't remember how this developed. I only remember the discomfort. There is always confrontation and nervous changeability with Gaskill.

His best productions are of plays that are essentially of themselves warm-hearted. Shakespeare, Farquhar, Chekhov have been the writers to whom he is best suited. For myself, I especially enjoyed his production of Osborne's *Epitaph for George Dillon,* the eclectic and magisterial production of *Three Sisters,* the promenade adaptation of Heathcote Williams' *The Speakers* for Joint Stock, another adaptation, in this case of Robert Tressell's *The Ragged Trousered Philanthropists,* and *The Recruiting Officer* for the National Theatre at the Old Vic. All these seemed to put him on his mettle and disarm him, give him courage and allow him to tap into his talent.

But it is perhaps as an artistic director that Gaskill has been as at his most original. His years at the Court theatre were immensely productive and were one of the most important episodes in the life of the post-war English theatre. His remarkable courage was instrumental in bringing the Lord Chamberlain's rule to an end, and he refused resolutely to programme to the critics' agenda. There was a shaky start to his directorship, which emulated Devine's opening season with a permanent company, but with a falling-off of the production standards. But he pulled things together and made remarkable conjunctions of old and new, developing the talents of emerging writers like Edward Bond, David Hare, Christopher Hampton, David Storey, EA Whitehead, Stephen Poliakoff, Heathcote Williams and Howard Brenton, as well as plays by Arnold Wesker, John Osborne, Charles Wood and Joe Orton. Threaded through these were often contentious and remarkable classical productions of Otway, Shakespeare, Chekhov, Webster, Ibsen, Brecht, Jarry, and Wedekind – all of them idiosyncratic and in healthy juxtaposition to the work of the National Theatre and the RSC. His appointment of Helen Montagu as General Manager and Nicholas Wright to set up the Theatre Upstairs was typical of many daring and original promotions which proved very successful and out of the ordinary. He produced the D H Lawrence season, a notable Osborne season, and a Bond season. He developed Keith Johnstone, and Bill Bryden set down the beginnings of work he was to develop later at the Cottesloe. David Hockney did his first stage design, for *Ubu Roi*, and the Court forged a relationship with a remarkable group of actors uniquely at home there. Through Gaskill's enthusiasm for all these people, the Court became one of the touchstones of London in the Sixties.

• • • • • •

Histories of the theatre are notoriously difficult undertakings, since apart from available texts, they depend so much on anecdote, recollection and journalism as sources about performance.

I am aware, in trying to set the *Chalk Circle* diary in context, of my rather Catholic need to connect things up. I am aware too, and significantly, that there was in the Sixties a sense of the possibilities of emancipation and that this emancipation was dependent on those who went before, particularly on those in the recent past, in the half century or so that was just gone. And that it perhaps brought with it a duty to them.

The difference between political advance and cultural regression in Britain has never been properly processed or understood. The wound inflicted by the Puritan revolution has been marked in the theatre by its making a final cutting-off from an art which even before that was already dislocated from its Shakespearean past.

The Restoration theatre, for all its fun and sophistication, is a costive reflection of a compromised world. The subsequent glorious revolution, with all its claim of being the foundation for modern British political life, eventually ushers in a theatre left to its own devices, dictated to by commercial imperatives and by political censorship, while, like the novel, it tries to express something that is more than rhetorical, in a world dominated by the gentleman artist and by modern British philistinism, where the poet retreats into the study, and the university sets the tone. Its modern history is one marked by brave ventures often outside the mainstream to return the theatre to something of its serious destiny, until the Second World War ushers in the possibility of a theatre free from many of its old restrictions and funded to express itself.

What we have made of this emancipation which, at the time of the diary, was being first realised, is difficult to assess, particularly at present when the theatre is jostling for position like a pitching ad man amidst all the cultural relativism, with the serious theatre finding itself fighting for breath and of its nature opposed to the values proposed by the renaissance of a purulent capitalism. There is always struggle, it seems.

After *The Chalk Circle* I continued to work as an actor in films, theatre and on television until in 1965 I was given a job as an assistant director by Anthony Page at the Court, and soon after I had my first play put on and directed my first play too, but I don't have a diary of things there.

Index